BLACK BOYS LIKE ME

CONFRONTATIONS WITH RACE, IDENTITY, AND BELONGING

MATTHEW R. MORRIS

VIKING

VIKING

an imprint of Penguin Canada, a division of Penguin Random House Canada Limited

Canada • USA • UK • Ireland • Australia • New Zealand • India • South Africa • China

First published 2024

www.penguinrandomhouse.ca

LIBRARY AND ARCHIVES CANADA CATALOGUING IN PUBLICATION

Title: Black boys like me : confrontations with race, identity, and belonging /
Matthew R. Morris.
Names: Morris, Matthew R., author.
Identifiers: Canadiana (print) 20230150381 | Canadiana (ebook) 20230150489 |
ISBN 9780735244580
(hardcover) | ISBN 9780735244597 (EPUB)
Subjects: LCSH: Morris, Matthew R. | LCSH: Black people—Race identity. |
LCSH: Race awareness. |
LCSH: Black people—Race identity—Canada. | LCSH: Race awareness—Canada. |
LCSH: Black people—
Biography. | CSH: Black Canadians—Biography. | LCGFT: Autobiographies.
Classification: LCC FC106.B6 M67 2024 | DDC 305.896/071—dc23

Book design by Dylan Browne
Cover design and art by Lisa Jager

Printed in the United States of America

10 9 8 7 6 5 4 3 2 1

Penguin
Random House
VIKING CANADA

Mom, you've always understood. But I hope this makes things a little bit clearer. Love always.

"I will offer you my heart. I will offer you my head. I will offer you my body, my imagination, and my memory. I will ask you to give us a chance at a more meaningful process of healing."

—KIESE LAYMON, *Heavy*

CONTENTS

HOW LONG IS THIS NIGGA SPENDING ON THE INTRO?

I thought everything would be different. Everything.

As much guidance as I got, I thought I'd have more. Or at least enough to get me to the point where I no longer needed direction. I didn't realize that with every step I took along the way, I was being watched. If I'd known that, I might have done certain things differently.

Who would have thought that decisions made over toys at Christmas, albums bought on birthdays, and minimum-wage jobs would shape the entirety of a grown man's life? How could I foresee that the way my hair grew out of my head would eventually make it easier for me to paint my own skin? I'm not a boy anymore, so I understand why I didn't consider those questions back then.

When you blend love with race and manhood and pain over a period of time, many bits of it become hard to digest. Mom inevitably found it too tough to stomach. I think Pops did too. Some of the questions I had to face left me disoriented. Thinking about it now, I don't know when I was taught to question. But my circumstances required it.

I'm not an expert in anything but my own experience. I've learned to take shallow heed in seeing things from the outside looking in. I'm also cautious about observing things from the inside looking out. Instead, safety finds me when I stay still, in the dead centre, and look around. My learning is not deeply rooted in reading about what Black boys like me endured. My thoughts are more tethered to the fuckery me and Black boys I knew dealt with. This is some "One Mic" shit Nas rapped about in '01. And in ten years, I might disagree with parts of this book's message. But probably not. This shit bangs because for so long the same shit banged about in me. These are moments that seared themselves into my lungs, my heart, my head, my muscles. And everything else inside.

My earliest memory is of my first day in junior kindergarten. I don't remember getting dressed or who walked me the short distance from our house on Parsell Square to Lucy Maud Montgomery Public School. The faces are now a blur, but there were a lot of them. I put my little knapsack where I was told to, and I sat on the carpet with the rest of my new classmates. A wave of uncertainty washed over my entire body. This unknown space terrified me down to the bone. I knew that I wouldn't be able to survive the day there. I needed to escape.

Questions tugged at my brain. Why did I feel so cornered, so small? I now know that the questions I was trying to tease out were: How could I gain a sense of personal control in a room where I held no power? What would happen if this uncomfortable feeling that I did not belong continued to torment my insides? Back then, I merely wondered, Why does it feel so awful here? I couldn't cry. Several other children were trying that strategy, and they were met with Kleenexes and gentle rubs on the back. Was there some way I could make myself invisible? I sat motionless, cross-legged on the threadbare grey, red, and blue carpet. Eyes glazed and hands tightly tucked between my thighs, hoping that no one would talk to me or even look in my direction. I knew that wouldn't be enough.

I came up with an idea so simple yet interwoven with what I was feeling in that moment that I had to tell myself that it wasn't just an idea but a reality. A gut reaction to what I was emotionally experiencing, so visceral that it had to be true. An idea that scraped at my sense of right and wrong, of good and bad boys. A play that, if successful, would make me safer but threatened who I considered myself to be. I weighed my options, thought about the questions I still had in my head, and got up from the carpet.

"Miss . . . Miss." I motioned to the teacher. "I need to talk to you," I said as I walked to the cubby space where I had put down my backpack earlier.

"Yes, um, Michae—Matthew? What do you want to talk to me about?" She had the sweet and endearing tone that only kindergarten teachers and grandmothers possess. She looked into my eyes the way that only kindergarten teachers and grandmothers do.

"My stomach is really hurting me and so is my head. So bad. I feel a bit dizzy and feel like I might throw up. Miss, I don't want to throw up. I just don't feel good at all," I said, laying it on thick. Knowing that this one act, this one performance, this one conversation with the person who held all the power would determine if I would have to endure my all-consuming fear for the rest of the day. My fears were all I could think about. I had to make this work. I had to be a bad boy in order to get what I needed.

"Oh no, that's not good . . . Malc—Matthew. That's not good." She looked into my eyes and waited for me to reply.

"Yeah, Miss. It's not. And I really want to stay here because I love it and it's my first day and I'm so sad, but I feel so bad right now. I mean I feel so sick right now. I don't know why. I wish I just felt better, but I'm not feeling any better, and I might barf. I'm going to barf. I don't want to barf on the first day. I don't want to barf here. Miss, can you please help me? Please, Miss."

Looking up at her, I thought of everything from eating Brussels sprouts to drinking spoiled milk to watching the washing machine in my dark basement going round and round. The idea I had was no longer an idea but a feeling. It had to be. I made myself feel it. I stared at her and allowed my eyes to get as wet as they could without crying. Crying could possibly blow it, I thought. I needed to be weak but strong. Passive but present. Bit of a boy but a bit of a man.

"Okay, Mart—Matthew." I kept my eyes fixed on the shoelaces my father had recently taught me how to tie. "Mom is coming to pick you up, okay? Just sit here. This is going to be your cubby for the year, Matthew, okay? Maybe ask Mom to make you some chicken soup when you get home, alright?" I kept my head down to avoid her seeing any glimpse of joy or deceit or relief. "This is *my* cubby, Miss? Okay, I'll tell her about the soup. I'm sorry, Miss."

She gently rubbed my back and walked away. I kept my head down and waited for Mom.

When we walked in the front door, I didn't wait to be told to sit on the couch. I knew not to even attempt to pick up the TV remote. I was under a different power now, and I was in no position to abuse it. Plus, I still had a character to play. Mom came into the living room and put a blanket over my shoulders and looked long into my eyes. They were still wet. Hers were a bit too. She stared at me for what felt like thirty hours and then walked away into the kitchen.

The blanket over my shoulders was so warm that sweat beaded and ran from the top of my forehead down toward my eyebrows. I watched my little baby brother scramble after toys on the floor. I no longer wished I was invisible: I wished I was telepathic like my favourite X-Men character, Professor X. Squeezing my concentration in his direction, at his legs, trying to will him to walk over to me and peel off my blanket wasn't working. Not able to be invisible, not capable of using my mind to control others, I left the sweat dripping from my scalp, and I reclined deep into the couch, having learned that sometimes being a bad boy paid off. Not understanding how this itty-bitty idea that my four-year-old brain came up with in order to feel safe in my surroundings would eventually be confounded by so many other things—most of all my Black skin.

"Here's your chicken noodle soup that your *teacher* recommended, Matthew," Mom said as she came from the kitchen cradling a steamy yellow bowl in her two strong ropey white hands. She looked at me as she gently put it down. "And you're going to eat it all. We don't waste anything in this family."

Thinking about it now, I don't know if she knew that I knew that she wasn't entirely convinced that I was actually sick. Whatever she thought, she didn't ask any questions. And I ate every last morsel of that bowl of soup. I didn't want to disappoint Mom. And I had become so invested in my idea. Invested in the character I had created.

I had got myself home, to the one place I felt safe. With Mom. And I think she knew that in that moment I needed love, safety, family, and time, which meant more than a day at school. So I ate the soup. And we hugged. And she told me to get better because I was going back to school tomorrow. I knew that I couldn't fake being sick to get home ever again.

I like to think that we both thought that, in some circumstances, being a good boy who plays bad is better than crying and telling the truth. Maybe it's even better than a bad boy playing good, especially when your skin is already tinted. Because sometimes the truth, for Black boys like me, is way harder to play straight. Sometimes, being a bit bad is easier than enduring the consequences of being honest with the outside world. Mom was thirty-nine when we looked eye to eye and came to that understanding. I didn't understand it then, but at four years old I felt it and moved forward. The rest is a reclamation to get right again. To see things full circle. To offer others a way to see things from where I stand, from the dead centre of the person I've become, looking around.

FOUR A.M. IN BROOKLYN

CHAPTER 1

Although I hadn't seen Tre since I left college midway through my sophomore year, I knew he'd be cool with me spending the night. But even though we were boys, I felt bad for the predicament I would be putting his girl, Kiera, in if I just ended up passing out in their apartment. Despite how late it was, I didn't want to begin the new year waking up on my boy's couch in Brooklyn when I had a hotel room in Manhattan. That would be some young boy shit. I was a grown man.

"Hopefully we'll see you tomorrow before you leave, Matthew. You should take a cab back though. It's mad late," Keira said as I put on my coat and used the door for balance while stepping into my Timberlands. I nodded.

"Yo, fam, hit me when you get to your telly," Tre said. "You should probably take a cab though, for real. You know these niggas don't take holidays off."

We both laughed. "I know, my nigga. I'm good. I'll hit you when I get back," I told him. "Yo, lock the door behind me. You know these niggas don't sleep."

The sidewalks were quiet and cold and messy and dark. Before I'd left, I checked on my phone where the nearest subway station was and then asked Tre for directions to make sure. Walking to the subway, I thought about how much me and him were boys. How he could have said things to me that were more emasculating but simultaneously more caring, like "Take a cab—this ain't Canada, my nigga." Instead, he said things that we both knew and loved and respected. I kept thinking about how we were once college roommates, then boys, and now men.

On my way to the Fulton Street station, I noticed a building with a blue emblem I had seen countless times before on vests, jackets, trucks, and in damn near half the movies I watched when I was a kid. I saw Denzel Washington wear it in *The Bone Collector*. I saw him wear it again as a crooked-ass cop in *Training Day*. Dude was yelling, "King Kong ain't got shit on me." I love Denzel. I loved that movie. But as I fixated on that emblem, I remembered all the crooked-ass white boys who donned it in a bunch of other movies.

The pictures in my mind as I walked by the police station were sobering. I felt my body for the first time in hours: I felt again that I was a Black man. It woke me. It forced me to be on alert, corrected my posture, coerced my stride and step. It redirected my wandering eyes. As I exhaled into the brisk Brooklyn winter air, I noticed I could see my breath, like smoke clouds, for the first time. The lightening sky reminded me of how many hours had passed since we'd all counted down in unison. As I followed the path through the days-old snow along the sidewalk, I made sure my walk masked the amount of Jameson I had indulged in. My gaze focused on the mix of commercial lofts and brownstone walk-ups that lined the street. I corrected the limp in my natural step as I calculated the exact tilt of my neck to ensure I did not look evasive or inquisitive. The stairs to the Fulton Street station appeared beyond some sidewalk ventilation grates yards in front of me. I had made it to my first stop.

Passing that police station felt like it took twenty days and revealed how my body has become fixed to my constant mental vigilance—still to this day. That short walk and the symbols I saw along the way signalled me to slip into survival mode. Walking past the police station to the subway station brought out an understanding of how my Black body has always been defined by things—precincts, platforms, proximity—and never been afforded the ability to define itself. Once I noticed that NYPD emblem, I felt myself lose autonomy over certain parts of my outside. It made me breathe deeper. It slowed my heartbeat. It turned my eyes stonelike and sent my guts up to the bottom of my throat. In the short distance between those two stations, I was compelled to be a different version of myself.

No cops were standing outside their little precinct that night, yet I still felt it necessary to stage my innocence. Doing anything less would jeopardize my safety. There was no audience in that darkness for what I have learned to perform and reperform, over and over. Dulling down my Blackness for the sake of my survival.

I stayed on my square the rest of the way to my hotel room. Even though I had ridden the subway in NYC a few times before, I had never ridden it at four something in the morning, tipsy and alone. The subway stop and C train felt familiar but not comfortably familiar. They were things I had seen countless times before—in Spike Lee joints, heard about them in dope documentaries about hip-hop graffiti, and even saw Angelina Jolie stop a train in *The Bone Collector*. I knew the story because I had long been in the audience.

But there was no encore that night.

The next morning, I thought about how I knew how I would have acted if I ran into other Black men who presented themselves in public the same way I did. Walking through the turnstile, I would have swiped my MetroCard—the one that a few days prior took me at least fifteen minutes to figure out how to purchase—with a nonchalant yet rushed demeanour so that anyone around me would have no question that I was from New York. I would have made sure no one saw my screen while Google Maps confirmed I was standing on the right platform, going the right way, waiting for the right train. For a variety of reasons, my hands would have been in my coat pockets. My eyes would have been on the move, darting around enough to let anyone interested in looking know that I fucking knew too. Just enough to let those people know that while I fucking knew, I definitely did not want to fucking play. All of us would have seen and noticed each other in a way that said we knew, even though we were unknown to each other. That morning, I thought about what I knew I would have done. I would have amplified my Blackness—for survival.

Everyone else on the subway would have been invisible to me. Behind the screen of real life in that real space of a real NYC subway, they would all be the audience.

How I acted while passing the police station and would have acted, if need be, on the subway were almost the same. Both performances were activated by two imagined audiences and had the same intention: to disarm any potential threat to my body. That is where the similarities end.

In front of that thin blue line, I leaned into a posture of innocence in order to avoid police perceptions of my potential criminality based merely on my skin colour. On that subway, I sloped into a posture that revealed the presumed dangers of Black bodies like mine. Both acts were unavoidable. And I don't know whether to feel sad or resentful because of that. Sad because Black bodies like mine are always fragmented to fit the targets of racism. Resentful because the forced splitting of myself leads to me involuntarily becoming the perpetrator of coded racial behaviour.

In one instance, I was the perceived threat simply due to my skin and clothing. In the other, I could have become threatened by my internalized racist reading of other Black bodies—the bodies that looked and dressed just like me.

But say I was on that subway car riding home and there was a group of young men near me speaking loudly to each other. I would have two completely opposite reactions depending on one thing.

The colour of their skin.

If they were white, Asian, or Latino, I would feel one way; if they were Black, I would feel another—regardless of things like tattoos or hairstyles or height or weight or belligerence or proximity. A group of white guys with full sleeves of tattoos would elicit a different emotion within me than a group of Black guys with the same sleeves. So what does that say about me?

When I, a Black man in his thirties, cross paths with an "urban-looking" Black man on a dimly lit street, my psyche whispers to me in almost the same way as a sixty-something white woman's would. When I observe a group of noisy young Black guys in a car beside me at a red light, I have the same degree of pause as a mid-forties white father of three. The only difference between me and aging Margaret or Tanner the dad is that I don't blatantly cross the street or grip the steering wheel with both hands while looking straight ahead with a starchy stare. Similar feelings, different reactions. Because I have walked down dark sidewalks as that *other* guy and been in the passenger seats of that *other* car.

Despite the twin murmurs Margaret, Tanner, and I all hear, I listen to something different. Something louder. Something inside me that says, That dude looks, walks, and dresses just like you, Matthew. So, you know what that means, right? The defendant can't also be the judge. He's committed the same alleged crime as you and pays for it daily. He understands his alleged crime, for better or worse, and acts in accordance with those perceptions and expectations. Just like you.

The humming becomes louder and louder the more I pay attention to the noise.

I think, Perceptions and expectations, Matthew. He puts them on himself because of what the world puts on him. Perceptions and expectations and performances. Passing by each other, it's impossible to know which came first. Just like you.

I listen to this voice, and I don't cross the street or shrink in my car or step away in an elevator.

As a teenager, I ignored these whispers so that I could take advantage. I had a keen understanding of how the Margarets and Tanners of the world felt around me. Even when they didn't explicitly show me, I could feel it. I knew how I felt around Black males like me on city buses or on the bleachers at high school basketball games. In high school, I leveraged my Black body anytime I took public transit. I would hop on the bus, head straight to the back, and sprawl out over some open seats. In an aisle seat, I splashed my duffle bag on the window seat, dipped my fitted cap just a bit lower than I normally wore it, slouched deep and extended one leg into the aisle, and turned up the music in my headphones.

I rode hundreds of buses, subways, and streetcars in Toronto as a teenager. Back and forth from school, football practice, the mall with my boys, Walmart for my part-time job, a girl's house to get my hair braided. On all those trips, there was rarely, almost never, a time in which someone would ask or even gesture for me to move over or pick my bag up off the empty seat. I hadn't even graduated high school and had already learned how racism could be exploited. The buses I took in Toronto as a teen showed me how I could use racism to my benefit. The subway I took at four a.m. in Brooklyn showed me that racism would never ultimately work to my advantage.

My performances on buses in Toronto and subway cars in Brooklyn were a form of cultural embezzlement. A loophole that

allowed me to steal from our cultural bank small means of comfort, of position. Only later did I find out that thieving such
currency just leaves Black boys like me even more indebted, in a
worse light. But it was what I was fed. Watching those crooked-
ass cops chase gangsta-ass niggas in movies set in New York and
Los Angeles. Absorbing it when news channels talked about
shootings and drug busts in my city and always ran a Black face
in their stories. Listening to my favourite artists rap about the
thug lifestyle. It fed me.

I consumed the idea of what it meant to be a nigga. I craved to
be him when I got on that 54 Lawrence East bus in Toronto's east
end. Only after my four a.m. subway ride in Brooklyn did I realize
that what I was being fed had consumed me. And I had been spit-
ting it out in a way that was fraudulent. Since my teen years, I had
vomited up too much of it. It's weird and scary because folks who
aren't Black appropriate Black culture all the time. When they do,
they're gently called racists. But some Black folks also embezzle
from Black culture these days. I pilfered my own image by taking
up all them seats on buses as a teen. I looted my own Blackness by
acting a certain way around imaginary Black bodies on midnight
subway runs and cold walks down dimly lit sidewalks. Cultural
embezzlement has me thinking these days. Thinking about the difference between cultural embezzlement and cultural appropriation.
What if there isn't a big difference between the two?

Even though I know I shouldn't, I look at other Black men and
make judgments about them, based on their aesthetic, and especially
if they are in groups. I can only imagine how I'd react if I encountered myself on that Harlem street at four a.m. on New Year's Day.
I would have passed me, that other Black man who clearly was not
afraid—at least on the surface. That bravado would be imposed over
a terrible insecurity about the unknown nightwalker, who just

happened to be as Black and equally aware of the body he was encountering—his own body.

Nevertheless, if I were to encounter me, I would be skeptical. Weary of the facades that people who look like me are forced to put on and which lead to that terrible feeling that wavers between fear and intent. I would fix my body in a state that was firm but not robotic. My mind would cross the street, but my body would be fully present to everything as my Timberland boots crunched the snow on the sidewalk. I would glance at the approaching man to see if I would be greeted with a head nod or a stare down.

Waddup, you good? I don't want no problems, but I also ain't worried about no problems, so if you stare at me, Imma stare at you. I may drop my eye contact first because I don't know this part of town, but you lucky. If this was where I'm from, I woulda never stopped staring because where I'm from, I know them parts better. I don't really know these parts like that, my nigga, so what's up, you good?

That would be the unspoken dialogue as we passed each other. And after we passed, pause. Deep breath.

And my Black ass, relieved and on the subway platform, swiping both the non-existent sweat from under my winter hat and my MetroCard, would say the same thing, regardless of how that moment between me and me went on the sidewalk. Black lives matter—they sure do.

But lately I've been asking more questions and uttering fewer statements. Questions like, Is everybody racist?

Black people can't be racist; woke ones know this. Right?

Racist people think other groups of people are inferior because of things like their skin tone and culture. Racist people discriminate and hold prejudice based on race. The latest evolution of the word *racism* includes the notion that racists operate out of bias and impact those they are biased against because of their power in society. Racism has been chiselled, then chiselled again, to the point where I don't even know who the racists are anymore. And I sometimes wonder if I'm one of them.

We've seemed to arrive at a racist world without any racists in it. These days, a racist earns their title by demonstrating unfounded bias against another group through the power they hold to make the lives of those they discriminate against harder. When juxtaposed with overt policies of the past, like separate water fountains and segregated seating on buses, it can seem like we've solved most of the issue. As if actions that spring from racist thoughts but have no power behind them aren't really racist. As if wielding unfounded bias toward another group isn't racism, just righteous disgruntlement. This new retooled racism can seem like a more accurate definition, even though it is still unfair to the people who have always been made to experience their race. It makes it even harder to pinpoint who and what is racist.

In middle school, I learned first-hand what a racist was: I'll call him Mr. Turner. He was a knuckle under five foot eleven with a face and frame coarsened by decades of weekend shinny and Labatt Blues. One of those middle-aged white guys who looked like he'd been styling his now-greying hair the same way since the early '80s and using too much P90 sunscreen on the bridge of his nose as soon as May rolled around. Mr. Turner was one of them good ol' Canadian-type racists from the '90s. Even though he lived in the city, Mr. Turner was the type of guy who didn't like all the pavement and busy intersections. It seemed to me that he found comfort in punching in and punching out, and then going home to watch *Hockey Night in Canada* with Don Cherry. Mr. Turner taught us different subjects, but it was the way he taught that helped me learn what a racist looked like.

Mr. Turner didn't make it hard to read between the lines. He never did anything flagrant but would make comments about arranged marriages to Fatima and Aaminah, and ask Abdi how long he'd lived in Canada. He told the Black boys to "pull our fucking pants up," and before even really knowing our names, he doubted we lived with both parents. A couple of times, before handing back a test I knew I did well on, he would fire off a few questions from the test at me because he thought I'd cheated. I wasn't looking for a "Congrats, you did well. You must have studied." But even if I were, I would have never gotten one from teachers like Mr. Turner and his friends. He acted surprised by me, never proud of me.

By the early 2000s, Mr. Turner and most of the white guys like him had retired from teaching in the schools where kids like me went. I graduated middle school having learned some indelible lessons from him and a few other teachers that didn't come from the textbooks we studied from. Lessons I hauled into high school classes and onto city transit buses and eventually onto NYC subway platforms.

But maybe it wasn't Mr. Turner's fault. Maybe the way the east end of Toronto used to look—his reality—clashed with what it had become in the late '90s. Maybe, in his middle-aged years, he ate up what I also began to chew on as a young Black teenager. When he talked to Aaminah and Fatima about arranged marriages, maybe he didn't know that that was some racist-ass shit to say to a thirteen-year-old Indian girl. And when he told us to pull up our pants, he for sure didn't realize that we never wanted to look or dress like him. Not ever. Maybe his actions toward us didn't reveal his actual thoughts about us.

Either way, I didn't run into too many racists like Mr. Turner after middle school. I don't know where those dudes are anymore, but I imagine they live at their cottages most of the year and don't say shit to me when they see me at the corner store or stop beside me at a red light. They just grip their steering wheels at ten and two and stare straight ahead, waiting for that light to change.

Mr. Turner taught me enough of what I needed to know about myself and how folks like him would always perceive me. My kindergarten teacher had taught me that "all people were created equal," and I'd heard that again in Bible study with my best friend, David Stone, in the sixth grade. But as an adult, in a room filled with middle-aged white men, I learned that what I thought I knew wasn't true. That "all people were created equal" thing has some caveats. The phrase itself is factual, but there are unspoken contradictions that spiral around it.

I used what I'd learned about my Blackness from movies and music to get two seats on the bus, but I didn't realize that doing that was what Mr. Turner had been implying about me that whole time in middle school. He wore wack shit but still had the audacity to tell me and my friends to pull up *our* pants. Mr. Turner and the rest of us looked at the plate differently, but we ate that same shit. And we both had reasons to. I feel like an asshole blaming him, but he was the one who kept the stove hot. He was the one who continued to offer it up without ever asking us if we wanted seconds.

I took small bites of the racism I was served. While I ate lightly—taking up extra seats or stealing the occasional pack of gum—some of my friends got gluttonous. I couldn't blame most of them for making decisions that seemed predetermined for them. And I definitely couldn't blame a friend like LeShawn.

I met LeShawn for the first time in the second grade. He trans-ferred to my school a few weeks into the start of the year, and we clicked by lunchtime on his first day. We both liked football and the WWF and the *X-Men* cartoon. He had just moved into a house right across the street from the school and right beside a small beat-down strip mall, which was convenient for him because he never came to school with a lunch. Instead of jaywalking right to his front door, LeShawn would jog over to the corner store in the

17

strip mall and buy some sour keys and a snack-sized bag of Hostess Hickory Sticks. I hated a lot of the lunches my mom made, especially toward the end of the week when I would open up my brown bag and pull out two slices of bread covered in margarine with no name cheese slices stuck between them. I wished I had enough change in my pocket, like LeShawn did, to be able to buy a bag of Hickory Sticks and some candy too.

LeShawn ended up moving away for a few years and came back to my school at the beginning of sixth grade. He was still short and stocky and dark and liked all the same things that I still did. Now we joked about other things, too, like how bad we got beat the night before or which girl was the baddest in class. He said he didn't like the white girls in our class, but we both spent hours after school making fun of Joel's head shape and big teeth only after Maureen decided to date him. Even though we were close friends, I never once was invited to his house. I didn't really want to be either. His front yard had the biggest collection of junk I had ever seen. His driveway had three or four dusty old cars that never moved. From twenty feet away, it was hard to see a path to his front door. Besides joking about who got beat worst, LeShawn didn't really talk about his family. I knew that he lived with his mom and that his older brother was away in prison. The only time he mentioned his dad was in sentences with the words *bitch* or *pussy* or *motherfucking piece of shit*.

We stayed friends but drifted a bit as the years went by and our circles grew. Once I was called to the office after he flipped a desk and stormed out of our middle school.

"Matthew, I know you are good friends with LeShawn, and he just needs someone that he trusts to go talk to him. He went to his house. Do you think you could go talk to him?" the vice-principal asked.

"Yeah, we boys, like boys, but I never really been to his house. Maybe he's just pissed. He'll probably come back," I said, knowing I didn't want anything whatsoever to do with the LeShawn I'd seen mad before.

LeShawn ended up coming back to school twenty minutes later with a baseball bat, but he seemed to cool off after bashing it against the dumpster beside the school a few times. Later that day, we talked about who was a better WWF wrestler, Shawn Michaels or Bret Hart.

By the time we got to high school, we had the same big circle of friends. We still spent time chopping it up whenever we would run into each other, walking to school or at football and rugby practices. We were still cool but not boys boys like we had been before. By eleventh grade, LeShawn was into rapping and playing dice during class, and I was focused on football, trying to get my ass out of Scarborough on an athletic scholarship. One of the last times I remember seeing LeShawn as a teenager was a late September day we hopped on the school bus to go play a football game against another high school.

It seemed like we had a decent-enough squad of athletes, but that season we just kept losing. Every bus ride to an away game started the same way. Everyone would be chatting about what had happened at school that day until the bus pulled out of the back parking lot. Then guys would put their headphones on and skip through their CD players, bobbing their heads slowly with eyes closed. After a few minutes, someone would pop a dubbed CD into someone else's portable stereo and play a track from Dipset or Nelly or the Hot Boys. When we noticed we were pulling into the opposing team's school, the music would get louder, and the songs would change. The whole bus would be screaming Jay-Z or DMX lyrics. When the bus and music both stopped, someone, catching that holy football ghost, would black out and start yelling about murder and banging heads and going crazy. Then we'd all grab our gear and exit the bus.

LeShawn had never seen this whole routine play out. On that September day when we hopped on the bus, Greg and a couple other guys debated which NFL team would win the Super Bowl.

"Yo, driva, can you open the door for a second, I got to take a piss," LeShawn asked lightheartedly. He exited the bus, and instead of going back inside the school, he stepped to the side of the building, pulled out his dick, and pissed on the wall right beside where the floor-to-ceiling cafeteria windows were.

"Yo, look at this lazy-ass nigga," Greg joked. "Can't even hold his bladder long enough to go inside. But always talking 'bout he a grown man." The whole bus came to the passenger side windows. The bus started hooting even harder when most of us noticed Mr. Ellins, Ms. Sawyer, and Mr. Nugent coming around the corner.

A few of us tried to warn LeShawn by yelling out the window. "Yo, L. We gotta roll, now!" He nudged his head a quarter ways around and gave the bus the middle finger.

The principal and his two vice-principals saw LeShawn. They waited until he was done and approaching the bus before they walked up to him. A few of us hopped off the bus when we realized that a conversation with a sixteen-year-old guy in football pads pissing on the side of the school was taking a lot longer than it should have. The principals didn't as much as blink in our direction before taking LeShawn inside.

Coach Burke hopped on the bus and said, "We've wasted enough time because one of you decided that taking a piss on the side of the school couldn't wait. Some of you are dumb as bricks, huh? Time to go."

We played "Murda Murda" by Ja Rule as we rolled into West Hill's parking lot that day. Greg was the one who blacked out after the music stopped. "These pussy-ass niggas ain't got shit on us. It's murda time, y'all. Let's do this!" he shouted. Two hours later we were back on the bus, quiet and our heads held low.

The next year I would see LeShawn sporadically around Scarborough but rarely ever at school. Greg told me that LeShawn got into an argument with an older guy from our area after the man said that LeShawn's mother sucked his dick for a twenty piece of crack cocaine. The next day, LeShawn shot the guy in the face with a .22 in broad daylight. The guy didn't die, and LeShawn went to prison for a few years. When he came home, he robbed corner stores and drug dealers. The high-risk takedown unit arrested him after a chase at the back of our old elementary school. I ran into him a few years after that and went to his new home for drinks. He had a pregnant girlfriend at the time. He told me how he had to surrender that night or else the police were going to kill him on the spot.

LeShawn was always a little bit shorter and a little bit darker than their ideal. His temper got him suspended enough times that it became normal to see LeShawn in the office or hear about him getting into trouble. While I was following the Black boy path that kept me inside classrooms, gyms, and on football fields, LeShawn was down another Black boy route we often saw come after years of Hickory Stick lunches and getting caught too often in the wrong place at the wrong time.

By our late teenage years, we followed tangible examples of Black manhood. We knew we couldn't colour too far outside the lines. That abstract work was for men like Jackson Pollock. LeShawn, me, Greg, and most Black boys who looked like us had to represent our bodies in a way that was realistic and representational. Our images would never be worth the canvas they were displayed on. Our expressions would never be deemed expression-ist. The picture was painted quite clearly for us.

It could have been me who hopped off the bus that day to piss. But I really, really wanted to make it to the NFL, so I'd pissed before getting on the bus. LeShawn should not have pissed on the wall right beside the big windows of the school cafeteria. He prob-ably should have just gone inside to our locker room and pissed in a toilet. We probably should have told him this instead of laughing when we saw the bricks between his legs become soaked with his urine. We probably should have taken that moment more seriously. Because, seriously, LeShawn could have been any of us.

That Black man. That ultimate threat. Even when peeing on the side of a wall. We are both innocent and guilty. We are both complex and simple. Complicated by how a simple infraction, like peeing on a wall, is used as evidence of a greater crime, instead of attesting to a biological need and youthful thoughtlessness. Simplified because the individual actions we take are reduced to a collective understanding that others have about us. Bystanders to society but somehow also complicit in its racism. Seen by others and ourselves as interchangeable objects.

I feel regret and responsibility for LeShawn and Greg and me and all the other Black boys like us. When I stare at my naked body in the bathroom mirror, I don't regret the tattoos I have accu-mulated since I started hopping on buses to go play football games against other high schools. Because those ornamentations I chose to permanently blot on my lighter Black skin could never mark me in the same way LeShawn had been marked from birth. I know my tattoos, which contrast with my pigmentation, add to my responsibility as a Black man. They somehow make me more Black and make me appear more dangerous, more criminal, more gang-ster. Something LeShawn had to inevitably face every time he got out of the shower after scrubbing his skin clean. Bus rides from

Scarborough to downtown Toronto and subway trips from Brooklyn to Manhattan have guilted me into accepting responsibility for appeasing other people's ideas about my body as a Black man. So, I embezzle more Blackness for the sake of correcting their eventual hindsight. My attempt to defy their expectations led me to accumulate more markers that epitomize the very thing I fight against. Strangers have never accepted the complexity of my personhood, my manhood, my Blackness. Neither have I.

Walking by the police station that night in Brooklyn forced me to act one way while walking into the subway station forced me to act completely differently. I wanted the police to see a respectable, harmless Black man. I wanted any Black men I encountered on the subway to view me as dangerous. I created a schism of my own Black masculinity based on my environment. I guess that's how fragile my Black masculinity is. Or maybe that is how pervasive racism is—so insidious that places that ping my "Blackness radar" provoke me to act in racist ways. Those commercials, shows, and movies, those late-night local news broadcasts, and all the sports and politics mindfucked me. For decades of my life, I thought that there was only one way to be a Black dude born and raised in the inner city. To this day, I still have to check myself from this thought when I'm out in public.

I have to check myself when I see a group of teenaged Black boys, and in the instant that I first see them standing there, I picture their hopes, desires for life, and present intentions in that time and space. I have to then reflect on where that picture in my mind comes from, and if it differs from the picture I see in the same situation with white boys. If my perception of those Black boys is more negative, I've pressed upon my own knotted racist thoughts.

Depending on the bodies involved, I conceptualize these two situations differently, seeing Black boys more negatively than white boys. And I may act differently depending on my context. These

23

subtle changes will be felt—especially by the Black boys. I know they will be felt by the Black boys because I felt them as a Black boy. And as a Black man, I've seen the knuckles of white women get even whiter as they grip their purses tightly beside me in an elevator. I've felt a similar tension in an elevator with my Black friends when a white guy enters. People *have* crossed the street on me for no other reason than how I look. Sometimes they do it while walking their Rottweiler, unaware that I'm scared shitless of dogs. A Rottweiler has never attacked me, but I just have a *feeling* about them based on my perception of them. Sadly, the dog-walker feels the same way about me as a Black man. It is all perception. And perception is powerful and it has real consequences. Suddenly I don't feel sorry for Mr. Turner at all.

Ironically, I *feel* racism and *act* on racist perceptions when I discriminate in certain situations: riding a NYC subway at four a.m., walking down a desolate sidewalk and passing other Black men at a time of night with a higher likelihood for some shit to go awry, and things like that. The feeling that things may go awry just because I am sharing a space with another Black body is merely my perception. But that perception begets a *real* feeling that I have. And feelings can foster actions, regardless of how subtle or explicit they are. Perception then becomes reality.

I could have and should have taken a cab back to my hotel that night in Brooklyn. Walking to the subway, I hated that the air was frigid, brittle. At four a.m., I felt guilty that I'd absorbed the lessons Mr. Turner taught me back in middle school. I pulled my pants up as I walked by the police headquarters and sagged them back down once I got closer to the subway. I remembered then that I forgot to use the bathroom before I left Tre's apartment. I thought about peeing against a wall, any wall, to relieve myself of the Jameson and ginger ale and ice cubes that pressed my bladder. My grown man bladder. But I told myself to hold tight just for a bit longer, because of everything I'd seen. Everything I'd learned. As I got on the subway and passed stop after stop on the way back to my hotel, it pained me to know that I was still awake while also knowing that *these niggas* don't sleep. Neither do the people who are always watching us.

The few blocks I had to walk from my subway stop to my hotel were safe. My only threat—the hustlers running a three-card monte scam—I had met earlier in the week after denying their innocent requests to participate in their hustle and offering them some liquor that I had brought down from my hotel room. They were safe to me because their performance was clear. They were safe because they performed near a hotel in a part of a town designed for people to visit. That hotel and those hustlers existed in a place for tourists and performers. That night, I had made it back—back into the audience.

All the fear and pain and shame and regret I felt on my way home dissolved when I slid my key card in to unlock my hotel room door. I didn't even bother brushing my teeth after I peed. That would have required me to look in the mirror. I went straight to sleep, proud. I survived.

DRIP OR DROWN

CHAPTER 2

Picture day landed rather early in the school calendar, falling near the end of September. We were experiencing an unusually balmy summer in Toronto, and the day was met with dry heat that pressed into the mid-thirties. I rinsed out my breakfast bowl in the sink and glanced at the clock on the stove: 7:47 a.m. Plenty of time to figure out a fit for photo day.

This isn't even for you, I thought, this is for the kids, your students. Put on whatever. You have thirteen minutes before you need to start thinking about leaving the house.

I thought about how dry the heat already felt and how meagre the air conditioners in my school were. This is for the kids. It really doesn't matter what you wear. You're the one off to the side, damn near out of focus, I thought, as I flicked through shirts in my closet. At 7:55 a.m. I settled on a plain white Izod T-shirt and jean shorts—a common stitch in my wardrobe.

I'd been teaching for a few years and had settled on a few wardrobe staples. On days I woke up feeling like a grown-up, I wore one of my Polo button-downs with black or blue slim-fit jeans. The single-button barrel cuffs that rested on my wrists in the morning would usually be rolled up to my elbow by midday, regardless of weather. As grown as I felt in my late twenties, I still couldn't get myself to feel whole in a casual shoe over a running one. My white and blue Nike Air Max 90s subtly matched the plaid tops I never tucked in. Short-sleeved Polos with distressed jeans and maybe a pair of Jordans were reserved for days when the reality of working as an elementary school teacher really sunk in. All workwear was accompanied by my jewellery: a Citizen watch I'd gotten as a Christmas gift, a gold Cuban link bracelet on the other wrist, and diamond earrings in both ears. And whether I decided to tuck them in or keep one out, I always wore three gold chains around my neck.

I pulled into the school parking lot a few minutes before eight thirty. When I stopped in the main office to grab my morning attendance folder, I noticed my principal staring at me.

"Are you seriously wearing jean shorts on picture day?"

I looked at him looking at me, and then I took a short second to look at myself. I hadn't thought much more about my clothes once I put them on, locked my front door, and left my house.

I looked down at myself again. "Yeah." I laughed. "It's over thirty degrees already, and it isn't even nine in the morning." I waved a good morning to the secretary and stepped toward my mailbox to grab my attendance sheet.

"When a parent in your class gets a copy of their child's class photo and they look at their child's teacher, what do you think their first impressions are going to be?" My principal had a way of trying to get his message across by asking a series of questions instead of simply stating his point. I regretted not answering his initial question in a weightier tone. I should have known that because he kept a tightly groomed moustache, rotated between three different pairs of Brooks Brothers slacks, and tucked in every shirt he ever wore, his question about my clothes was no joking matter—at least not for him.

The caffeine from my morning coffee had not fully kicked in, plus I didn't feel like getting any deeper into this hypocritical and absurd conversation to begin with, so I just stared at him, waiting for him to answer his own disrespectful-ass question.

"They may wonder what type of standards are set in the school their child attends. They may question the type of academic excellence that happens on a daily basis in their child's classroom. The small opportunities we get on days like today are our chance to send a message to our community. We don't have many opportunities to portray the image of our school to the public. Things like picture day are one of these moments."

I wanted to tell him to fuck off. I wanted to let him know that first off, he needed to get over himself and that his self-righteousness literally made me sick to my stomach. And that secondly he was merely a middle school principal, and he needed to wake the fuck up and realize that. Also that his moustache looked stupid on his stupid-looking face, and that I hated his Brooks Brothers slacks and random golf shirts, and that his suits were oversized and looked cheap and dated, and that he reminded me of one of those fake-ass, church-going hypocrites who judged everything and everyone but himself because he never took time to self-reflect. I wanted to tell him that maybe he should look in the mirror and worry about his sorry-looking ass instead of worrying about me and my jean shorts.

Instead I stared at him. Holding his gaze, I nodded, checked my mailbox, and left the office. We didn't share any other words. I walked to my classroom, dropped my bag and morning attendance down on my desk, walked back toward the school parking lot, got in my car, and drove home.

I looked through my closet for a pair of jeans that were suitable for a teacher in an elementary class photo.

All through morning announcements and first period, I itched in the clothing I had on. It had been years since I had mentally zoomed in on how my own clothing choices stitched to my job as a school teacher. I thought back to that Labour Day weekend when I accepted a job teaching the seventh grade. I drove an hour to an outlet mall in Niagara Falls to shop at Tommy Hilfiger. I didn't own any "teacher clothes" at the time, no clothes that I thought would suit a seventh-grade teacher. I bought khakis in all hues of autumn. I even bought a pair that were salmon-toned. I bought different plaid button-downs and golf shirts. I bought Sperrys from a SoftMoc store and boat shoes from the Old Navy beside it. I swiped my debit card at cash registers and turned that picture in my mind into a new wardrobe.

Over some time, I replaced the khakis with jeans, the Sperrys with Nikes, and the button-downs with extra-large hoodies or vintage tees. I was restoring the image of how I truly saw myself from the man I had pictured in my head that Labour Day weekend years and years ago.

I didn't just wake up one day and decide to show up for picture day wearing jean shorts. It took years to rediscover and feel comfortable with my own style and aesthetic while teaching, years before I became as comfortable as I first felt that picture day, leaving my house in jean shorts. For years and years, I had layered myself in fabric that concealed who I was. Coming to work in jean shorts, on picture day of all days, revealed the style—my style—that I had been working tirelessly to feel comfortable in.

After morning announcements, I stumbled my way through a history lesson about the coureurs des bois, French colonists who came to Canada before it was called Canada to trade European items with Indigenous Peoples for fur, which was a commodity in Europe. Europeans liked to wear fur as a symbol of prestige. The Europeans traded items of value to Europeans, like metal cooking utensils, guns, and gunpowder; they also traded cloth. They traded cloth for fur.

I had set up this whole interactive trading simulation activity for my students to participate in, but I just ended up talking. Talking about how Indigenous people had traded fur because the Europeans back then so badly wanted to wear it. I looked down at my denim pants. I thought about the temperature. It was ten something in the morning and probably thirty-three degrees.

The main office buzzed my classroom to let me know that the photographers were ready for us in the cafeteria. When we got down there, we waited outside the cafeteria doors for another class to wrap up their individual headshots. I tried to think about the rest of the morning and if I should continue with the history lesson or move on to math. My mind kept drifting back to the conversation with my principal. Was he right? Did jean shorts really diverge that far from jeans in conveying the academic excellence of our school? What did professional attire mean in a fucking elementary school? While the photographers were arranging students by height, the principal came in, looked me up and down, and walked over.

"Do you keep extra clothes in your classroom closet?"

"My car. The trunk," I lied. He smiled approvingly at me. As if he was a proud dad or something. As if he was my dad. As if he had taught me a lesson in the morning and saw me learn it less than two hours later.

"That's responsible. You know, years back . . ." His nauseating bullshit faded from my ear drums as I focused on how the photographers were arranging my students. The kids looked nice—scrubbed and bright. I wondered how much time and thought went into their outfits. They'd only had picture day a handful of times. This was a big deal for them. The clothes they picked to wear mattered, maybe bought special for the occasion. They probably thought about their clothes the night before. Maybe some of them were forced by their parents to wear things they didn't want to wear.

"... since then I have always kept an extra shirt at work," the principal finished, crowning his anecdote about spilling ketchup or coffee on himself with a final lesson. I half-smiled to convey my thanks for yet another lesson so early in the day. He patted my shoulder and walked away. My half smile said thank you. My eyes said fuck you. I hoped he could read them.

At lunch, most of the teachers gathered in the staff room to eat and chat about the morning. Warming my lunch up in the microwave, I noticed a teacher wearing cargo shorts and sandals. I wondered if the principal had talked to him too. I didn't ask. I guessed. I guessed that his receding hairline, dad tummy, and particular shade of skin made his shorts more appropriate than mine. Or maybe he just lived too far to drive all the way home.

I become uncomfortable when the folks I teach with talk to me about the clothes I wear to work. They use words like *flashy* and *stylish*, veiling the things they really want to tell me about my clothes. That's what it feels like. Comments that fester in the shade of questions like "Where did you get that hoodie from?" and "What is the brand of shoes you have on?" Peculiar questions that seem to stretch beyond the actual fabrics and materials.

These same folks never talk at the Tanners and Davids this way. When a colleague like Tanner comes to work wearing dress shoes, salmon-coloured slacks, and green argyle socks that subtly match his fitted button-down, they don't say he is *flashy*. They say he dresses well. To me they say, "Matthew, nice sneakers. What do *you* call those, 'kicks'? *Flashy*, man." I get itchy when they ask me and tell me about my clothes at the same time.

After a few years of teaching, I was both the most comfortable I'd ever been representing myself through the clothes I chose to wear on a daily basis, and the most chafed when my clothes became the topic of conversation.

I didn't understand. I was an elementary teacher in Scarborough, not an executive on Bay Street. Yet the closer I got to being comfortable in my clothes, the further I fell from being considered "professional" in this "casual" environment. I didn't understand. The closer I got to being comfortable in my skin, the more often my button-downs were replaced by T-shirts. The closer I came to feeling safe in knowing that I was a Black man, the more often my gold chains would lay outside my shirt, not inside. The more I understood how my role as a teacher fed my need to represent my true self in front of those kids, the more often those occasional slacks were replaced with distressed jeans and Nike Tech Fleece joggers. The Matthew Morris of Saturday afternoons was finally meshing with the Mr. Morris of the workweek. At least on the surface. I understood this to be a good thing. The gazes I felt on me told me that my understanding needed mending.

Perhaps I didn't understand what exactly *professionalism* meant. Or what *casual* attire meant in a professional context. Or what it meant to dress professionally in an environment where suits and dresses were not the custom. Or who came up with the rule book for non-professional professional attire. Or if we are all merely playing a high-stakes game of dress-up.

I figured out what game I was playing when I decided to go home to change from jean shorts to pants for the class photo. My principal reminded me of the rules. But I know he didn't make the rule book. So I went digging. Trying to find out who did. Finding out where words like *professional* and *casual* come from in the first place.

I learned that the term *professional* comes from folks who lived around the fourteenth century and spoke Middle English. Back in those days, as people started to specialize in a trade, they "professed" their skill to others and vowed to perform their trade to the highest standards. A person's reputation became fastened to their profession. Makes sense. The word *casual* arrived around the same time and was used to describe an occurrence that was "produced by chance." The definition of *casual* then loosened to also describe folks who were not to be depended on, "unmethodical" folks. *Professional* was tied to one's reputation; *casual* was too. Both words were used to describe a person. One did so positively; the other, not so much.

I wonder, back then, who prescribed the describing? I wonder which people were able to profess their craft? I wonder if much has changed? It seems as if our roles in contemporary culture have evolved, but the words we use to describe them haven't evolved at the same pace. There still seem to be fixed definitions of words like *casual* and *professional*, for *casual* and *professional* dress, even though there are now many meanings for many different people.

Although the shades of folk who work within our established professions have slowly mushroomed over our lifetime, the rule book maintains historical and subjective boundaries. It reinforces certain aesthetics and devalues others. And this rule book is indelibly written in black and white.

Still, how are the Jordans I chose to wear to work less professional than the boat shoes Tanner rocked? Both can be the same colour; both can be made of the same material. One denotes sailboats and yachting and therefore money. The other denotes sport and competition and therefore money. Maybe the difference between the two styles of shoe comes down to the two feet that put them on. Maybe the distinction is really two sides of the same coin. Boat shoes denote the *right* kind of money—the established, inherited kind. My kicks represent the wrong kind of money— the *flashy*, unfamiliar kind. The new portrait on the $10 bill will always be dwarfed in comparison to aged currency, like my low-cut Nikes compared to those Sperrys. I guess the currency we carry exists not only in the pockets of our pants but also in the pants themselves.

I like to think that I put on my "big boy pants" at nine months old. That's when I first learned how to place my naked belly button on the top of the playpen and contort myself over the edge of it—I had learned to escape. Years later, my father told me about the day that he folded up that playpen forever. While cooking dinner for my mom and me, he noticed out of the corner of his eye, his first-born son wearing nothing but a saggy diaper standing at the edge of the kitchen. He said that he walked over to me, picked up my little diaper-draped body, and put me back in the playpen. He then watched me from behind the kitchen wall. When I repeated the same manoeuvre again, he folded up that playpen and put clothes on me. In 1986, at nine months old, I had already branded myself as a kid that people needed to keep an eye on.

Around that same time, a clothing brand crawled its way toward fashion royalty. A driven, creative boy named Ralph Lifshitz, who was born decades before me to Ashkenazi Jews from Belarus, grew up just like me, a few hundred miles away in a poor neighbourhood in the Bronx. While I was nakedly toppling out of the playpen by the mid-1980s, he was treading a track that caught a lot of people's attention.

Like me, Ralph took steps to alter his persona, changing his last name from Lifshitz to Lauren. Like me, Ralph Lauren was raised by immigrants. Like me, he didn't know about the sporting game of polo. Unlike me, he knew that this game was synonymous with elitism. Perhaps like me, he dreamed of high class and wealth. By the time I went home to change out of the Polo jean shorts that Ralph Lauren once dreamed about and then made in 2016, he had turned his company into a brand that capitalized on my fantasies. His clothes reminded me of who I thought I was, in

MATTHEW R. MORRIS

a way that modelled who I dreamed of being: a man with money and success.

Polo capitalized on the fantasy that you are what you wear. Throughout the 1980s, if you wore Polo, you had money and belonged to a select group. Among fashion brands, Polo fell just under the luxurious ranks of Louis Vuitton and Gucci. As his company grew, Lauren came out with different branches of the brand, including Polo Sport; each branch was based on the company's upper-echelon aesthetic. But with Polo Sport and the growing popularity of the Polo brand, all that changed. Lauren's company saw changes in its customer base. The Polo *narrative* did not change, but the people who were now wearing it surely did. The Black community got a hold of it. Polo gained some extra horse-power; however, this new consumer demographic also changed the way society saw the company.

When Black people started wearing Polo, especially in the hoods of New York City, Los Angeles, and Atlanta, they altered the way Polo was received, marketed, and consumed by the public. Polo still carried the connotations of wealthy and elite, but it was also being worn by the broke and Black.

The sartorial aesthetic created by Ralph Lauren survived the demographic shift and maintained its status as a brand while simultaneously creating an alternative meaning—with the same clothes. You had preppy white boys wearing Polo knits to Christmas parties in Richmond Hill and Black kids wearing the same knits to basement jams in the "ghettos" of Scarborough and Rexdale. The brand spoke one meaning to two contrasting populations. By wearing Polo, two different groups—rich white and poor Black—signalled their aspirations through the aesthetic appeal of wealth, of having money, of being "up there." Wearing the same clothes, one group maintained its elite status while the other dragged Polo to the depths of the urban. It is hard to define the complexities of what it

36

means to dress *urban* without stereotypical images of baggy jeans, basketball sneakers, and jewellery. But urban dress is much more nuanced than that.

It isn't so much about the clothes themselves but rather *how* they are worn. My urban style lies more in the untucked appearance of an expensive button-up or the slight sagging of jeans than the actual brands. About two decades after its birth, Polo meant conservative and ghetto at the same time; it became a clothing company with double meanings, distinguished by the colour of the skin covered by that Polo logo.

I went to the ATM machine to take out $200 before our coach bus left the mall parking lot. The school lunch lady, Jade, and the secretary, Joanna, had been planning this Casino Rama trip for a few months. I had already paid the fee to take part, but I had a bigger goal. I wanted to flip my $200 into a couple thousand and give the cash straight to Kyle's mom, Patricia, who was also on the bus with us. Every teacher, student, and adult in the building loved Kyle. Patricia had two boys, and Kyle was the youngest. Jade and Joanna had organized the casino trip because Kyle needed life-saving brain surgery and Patricia couldn't pay the associated medical costs. And he was in my class. Kyle slurred his words when he talked and had an oversized head and never really grasped any games we played in gym class. He hung on to a few math lessons but wrote and reasoned like a second grader when it came to storytelling. I always found it weird that he, a fifth grader, got upset when he wasn't first in line to head out for recess. But I had only been teaching full-time for three years. I was still wearing khakis bought from Tommy Hilfiger and boat shoes more often than Nikes. I had compassion for Kyle.

I went to the ATM to take out $200 because that was a lot to me as a twenty-seven-year-old elementary teacher and I wanted to be generous, and also because I had cut Kyle from the junior basketball team two weeks prior for double dribbling all the time and moving like he had two left feet. So I took out the money in hopes of doubling it and professing my character to the older teachers and staff by giving Patricia my winnings on the bus later that night. At least those were my plans.

The roulette table at Casino Rama didn't know me or Kyle or Patricia or Jade or Joanna, and it told me that rather flatly. After about thirty minutes of gambling, I walked my last two Viola Desmonds to the bar and waited for the bartender to see me.

He didn't.

I sat up straight on the bar stool, turned my hat backwards to expose more of my forehead and face, cleared my throat even though I didn't need to, and adjusted my watch while placing my elbows outright on the bar.

He still didn't see me.

I stared at him straight in his eyes on the second or third time he walked past me behind the bar. I cleared my throat again. When he dashed off past me to dish ice into another clanking cup, I said my order. "Double shot of Canadian Club with a splash of ginger ale."

No response.

I was talking to no one. I was talking to myself. I was echoing off the mirrored backsplash behind the bottles on the back wall. I took my elbows off the bar. I felt awkward for slouching a bit. I looked down, fixed my watch again, and waited. Waited for someone to notice me. To take my order. To see me.

Nothing. I sat there trying to figure out how to coerce someone behind the bar to actually see me. Apparently I was invisible. For a second I thought about putting my belly button on the edge of the bar and flipping over it to pour my own drink. But too many eyes would have been on me if I did that, and I wasn't a baby anymore. I was a grown man. So I waited.

An older white man took a seat on the bar stool right beside me. We made eye contact and politely nodded at each other. "Roulette, man. It's cruel. The number I had been playing all night hit right after I decided to get up because I had lost enough money already," I said. "And I swear this isn't the first time that's happened to me," I continued, because I needed someone to see me.

"Oh, brother, I know," he said. "Down two grand and I've only been here ninety minutes."

"What's your game?"

"Craps. Used to have beginner's luck. Not lately."

I didn't know how to play craps. For the longest time I thought the game of craps was actually called crabs.

"So damn chilly in here," I said. "And the way they got the air blowing in, you could be up in here until three in the morning and think it isn't even close to midnight yet. Warm as hell outside, but at least it's not raining tonight."

Weather. I always pivot to weather in the absence of a true conversation.

"I know," the older white man obliged. "Supposed to get a downpour on Monday though."

The small talk fattened a bit as I forgot about that double shot of Canadian Club with a splash of ginger ale I had wanted to order over twenty-five minutes ago. Me and the older white man talked about how the Buffalo Bills were doing—what they've always done since the Jim Kelly and Thurman Thomas days—then teased on about the Raptors signing Lou Williams and how Kyle Lowry finally looked like an All-Star.

"That's a nice watch you got on. Very clean," I said. His watch caught my attention as we went back and forth about sports and casino gambling. It looked like one of those watches my favourite rappers brandished in music videos when they rhymed phrases like "Rollies" and "wrist clock" with sounds like "tick tock."

"That's not a Rolex, is it?"

He blushed at the compliment. "A Breitling. It is one of their cleaner ones. Thanks, man."

I always felt slightly awkward when older white guys talking to me ended their sentences with *man*. But on this occasion I didn't draw back like I normally would have. I moved my left wrist back onto the bar and fixed myself up on the bar stool.

The older white man didn't care to return the volley by commenting on my watch.

"What are you drinking?" he asked instead.

"Canadian Club double. Splash of ginger." Bond, James Bond. I looked at him, then the mirror in the backsplash, and wondered if my spine was as upright as it could be. And I wondered what he thought of the $300 Citizen I had on my left wrist.

"You?" I said.

He told me he was drinking brandy, but he noted that it was not the shitty brandy like Rémy. I mentioned that I enjoyed the taste of cognacs like Hennessy but preferred to drink whiskys like Canadian Club. I was lying. But he didn't know, and I didn't divulge that I thought spending $60 on a bottle made no sense when you could spend $40 and get the same drunk if you finished it, regardless of the brand.

We shifted our conversation to the difference in quality between watches, wines, and wagers. Then the older white man said something that pressed itself onto my brain.

"You can tell a lot about a man by two things: his watch and his shoes."

You can tell a lot about a man by two things: his watch and his shoes . . .

In the middle of the summer, Casino Rama had both air conditioning and extra oxygen blowing full tilt. The older white man, who was easily near the same age as my own father, proceeded to leverage his chips into the position of fatherly advice. While he waited to order his brandy and me my whisky, he offered suggestions about how to navigate society by negotiating worth with others. Though he was clearly older and I was clearly younger, though he was WASPy white while I was paddled Black, he spoke at me through those two themes: watches and shoes. Watches and shoes, I guess, do tell us a lot.

Clearly I felt this way, too, on some level, since I was the one who'd turned the slim convo into a plumper one by commenting on his watch. Clearly he considered me worthy enough to engage in a conversation about aesthetics and values and tastes, although when I raised my left wrist with its Citizen watch and right wrist with its gold Cuban link bracelet back onto the bar, he mentioned nothing. While he was talking, I wondered to myself, If I had the same watch and the same shoes as this man, would I be "worth" as much as him out there in the "real world"?

"So, how much does one of those cost?" I asked. I could have done a Google search on the bus later that night, but my earlier plans of doubling my money and showing Patricia how much I cared about Kyle had dried up. I wasn't in the mood to plan or dream at that point in the night. I wanted to learn. Why not be taught more by this older white man? I was sitting here, thirsty, anyway.

A brief interruption by the bartender gave me my answer. An answer I already knew. Although I had arrived at the rather empty bar some thirty-odd minutes before this man, he was asked what his order would be at the same time as me. Before that, I had been ignored. I was clearly second. In a way, it indicated that things like watches and shoes mattered—as does who wears them. Although the bartender couldn't see the man's shoes and most likely didn't have the time to notice his watch, or mine, he was served first. All this bartender could see on that summer evening was two men, seated at the bar.

We were both wearing Polo.

Maybe I wasn't much like Ralph Lauren after all. After all, men with skin like mine have been treated differently all along. All the while we tried to keep up by wearing the same clothes as them. Didn't mean a thing. They tied ropes around the necks of suit-wearing Blacks and dropped them off branches only a half century ago. The string that ties clothing to race extends even further back.

Most of the suit-wearing Black men who were lynched between the 1880s and 1960s weren't really suspected of taboo charges like having sex with white women. No, those charges were a strategy to regulate and restrict Black citizenship and individuality. Lynching was done to maintain boundaries and anchor statuses. Them suit-wearing Black folks who got lynched were business owners and farmers competing economically with the whites, and they were Blacks who "passed" as white. The names of the Black men's tailors didn't matter to them white audiences back then. Today, the double reading of the Polo brand reveals how heavy the stain of Blackness still is. Our fabrics are a strange fruit, indeed.

How we see clothing stretches even further back, supposedly to the beginning of time for some. Way back in the day, a chap named Adam met a lovely woman named Eve in a heavenly garden. Things were supposedly perfect. Until, of course, some shit went down and things got fucked up. Some snaky-ass creature rolled up and started politickin' with Eve. He told her about a dope spot to get some free eats, and she unfortunately followed that snake's advice. I think Adam went too. She gobbled down some apple, and all hell broke loose after that. Until then, these two humans had no idea about shame, embarrassment, pride, or anything of the sort. Once they ate that forbidden fruit, the big man upstairs made them "woke." And one of the first things they noticed were their naked bodies. So Adam and Eve scrambled for the earliest fabric.

And since then, we—and our images—have become distorted through hierarchies of materialism. Some of our simplest modesties, like clothes, have become markers of differences and values. Whether it was leaves then or logos now, clothing is just another item used to tear us apart.

When I wear a pair of jean shorts to picture day, I am questioned about my professionalism as a teacher and about the image I am portraying to the community I serve. I am pressured to change myself. When self-made millionaires in Silicon Valley wear yellow-tinged, bacon-necked T-shirts for television interviews on *60 Minutes* and *MSNBC Live*, signalling the changing of the old guard through their apparel, they are applauded. When professional basketball players wear clothes to work that express how their culture has also evolved, they are chastised. Bay Street white-collar brokers employing their business skills in casual attire have become the norm, while what Raptors point guards wear to employ their skills in a *gym* is mandated by the NBA. They must dress in business or conservative attire while arriving to and departing from scheduled games. Seems a little off, doesn't it? Since both, by the way, are self-made millionaires.

When nineteen-year-old white kids wear khakis, they are looked at as "college kids." When nineteen-year-old Black kids—especially the ones from California—wear khakis, they are looked at as "gang-bangers." When that young white boy combs the majority of his hair to one side of his head, he looks cute, like a young businessman. When that young Black boy gets a part in the side of his haircut, he looks like *one of them* rappers or *some typa* thug. When that fourteen-year-old white guy grows his hair out long, he is "coming of age" and "finding himself." When that fourteen-year-old Black guy grows his hair, well, Would you look at that teenager with his Afro and that one with the braids? How outrageous is that? Doesn't he have parents? That kid needs to grow up and do something about his hair.

Why? Because it grows like a thicker fabric that is a little rougher on our skin? What has you so itchy? Is it my style, or is it me?

I also wore a T-shirt to picture day, but my shorts drew attention from my superior. You would think that he would find it more unbecoming to see my tattooed arms exposed than my legs. I can only think that my T-shirt and jean shorts became unprofessional, urban, and ghetto all at the same time because too much of my skin was showing.

A little less than an hour later, I was thanked for covering up. No one ever told me why Chris's cargo shorts and sandals were just fine to wear for his class photo. I thought I had left the teachers like Mr. Turner behind when I graduated from middle school. Instead I learned that the Mr. Turner types have changed in name only.

It seems that my clothes never quite fit me. Once I pop the tag off that shirt or those jeans, their value is less than what I paid at the cash register. The fabrics depreciate when I put them on. Sometimes before leaving my home, I spend extra time looking in the mirror by the front door. Not to adjust how my shirt sits on my shoulders or how my pant cuff sits on the tongue of my shoe, but to mentally prepare myself and try not to think about what I know my colleagues will think when they first see me. When I look back at myself, I cringe a bit knowing that certain readings of who I am are made simply because of what I wear. And that the clothes I wear are refashioned by the skin I'm in.

Clothes don't mean shit until we put them on. It's the fabric of our society that sells us the meaning behind the cloth that adorns us. Even if you can tell a lot about a man by two things, his watch and his shoes, my shoes carry less value if my feet are wearing them.

My watch is simply something that tells me that the time today is the same as the time it was way back then—back when niggas got lynched while wearing the same suits as the white audiences who watched, and further back to when those first folks used fig trees to cover their bare skin.

I should stop taking those extra moments to look at my reflection without reckoning with what I see. Stop trying to line up my view of myself with outsiders' gazes. Maybe that will help me see things a little clearer. I mean, my principal questioned me about my choice to wear jean shorts to a class photo. At least he didn't tell me to pull my pants up.

IF YOU'RE READING THIS, IT MAY BE TOO LATE

Looking back now, I don't know what Mom was thinking. Maybe she'd noticed that he was becoming one of the most recognizable Black faces of the early 1990s. Or maybe she had asked her white nephews what they thought her Black son wanted for his ninth birthday. My cousins were older and in high school. The music that boomed from the speakers in the trunk of their gold Oldsmobile Cutlass Ciera as well as the in-ground basketball hoop that stood, regulation height, on the edge of their parents' driveway were behind my subtle idolatry of them. They lived in Scarborough too; however, their environment at home was a bit different than mine. They lived with Mom's brother and his wife—my white uncle and auntie. Visiting their house left me with the understated impression that for them, certain song and sport were more of an escape rather than, as they were for me, an entry point. Still, no matter how much white families tried to protect their children's minds from Black culture in the mid-'90s, in places like Scarborough, it was impossible to prevent the daily infiltration of at least a little bit of Blackness. Maybe that's what Mom was thinking: if even the white kids in Scarborough were swaying toward this hip-hop thing, buying her Black son a hip-hop cassette wasn't such a bad idea.

On Labour Day weekend, before my birthday and the start of grade four, I walked with Mom to Cedarbrae Mall. She no longer made me hold her hand while crossing main intersections, so crossing Lawrence Avenue East at Markham Road beside her, but not attached to her, made me smile. She made me feel like I was no longer just a kid.

When we stepped through the mall's east entrance, the first store I saw was Sunrise Records. Mom told me that I could pick out one cassette tape that day and one more in a week, on my actual birthday. She liked to stretch out her money the same way we stretched out almost empty tubes of toothpaste and jars of peanut butter.

I knew that Mom knew which album I was going to pick. But I still don't know how she knew that I knew who the biggest, baddest, Blackest nigga in North America was at the time. It was like her soul figured out my Blackness before I did. Like she understood ways to protect me before I even knew how to protect myself. Me, oblivious to the complexity I would face due to my complexion. Her, tender with unspoken guidance. I walked to the back corner of the store to the rap section. Scanning the titles, I saw a plethora of cassette tapes with Black faces on the covers. I was especially intrigued by one with an image of a child's face transposed onto a photo of brown apartment buildings with the title *Illmatic* splayed in the bottom-left corner. The artist's name, Nas, was in the top-right corner in blood red in a font that was half-gothic, half-graffiti. Nas seemed like a cool rap name, but the word *Illmatic* and the buildings were too foreign to me. I noticed another album with two Black guys on it, and its title reminded me of funny words like *onomatopoeia* and *supercalifragilisticexpialidocious*. This tape's title, *Southernplayalisticadillacmuzik*, spun my head. The outcasts on its cover looked like two heads on one body. At nine,

I was scared by the concept of conjoined twins, so I didn't listen to their sample track at the juke station.

The next tape I picked up popped with bright colours. The main figure on the cover was a half man, half Doberman dressed in jeans and a flannel shirt. He was straddling a yellow and red doghouse in front of a bright-red brick wall, reaching for a slim half dog, half woman who had her head tucked inside the doghouse, her back end exposed. Three other dogs peered over the top of the brick wall, white speech bubbles beside each of their snouts: "Why must I feel like dat?" "Why must I chase dat cat?" and "Nuttin' but da dog in me!!"

I glanced back at my mom. She was standing under a Pop and Soul cardboard sign dangling from the ceiling. She sang along to songs by the Weather Girls while tidying up on Saturday mornings, and I wondered if the Weather Girls sang pop and soul music. I wondered what the word *soul* even meant, and why a type of music would be labelled *soul* if everybody had one.

I looked back down at the tape in my hand and spotted a scary-looking ugly, old white man in military garb peering from a doorway in the red brick wall and holding a net. A black arrow pointed at him beneath the words: "Dat mean old dog catcha!" A little dog or cat called from the green grass at the bottom of the doorway: "Snoop is always on top of things!" "Ratta-tat-tat." *Snoop Doggy Dogg* was outlined in bold yellow-and-black script in the corner with *Doggystyle* etched in block letters along the top of the brick wall. The cover looked like a page in a comic book, and after studying it, I had to know what it was all about.

I glanced back at my mom, lingering in that section that I didn't understand. She wasn't watching me, which let me know I wasn't doing anything wrong. I pressed the dial to number eight on the sample booth. The first song wasn't a song; it was more like a scene out of a movie. I could picture it in my head: a bunch of

Black guys talking shit to each other in a dusty house with clouds of smoke filling the room. When Dad and his friends got to drankin' and smokin' on Friday nights, they sounded just like Snoop and his friends did on the track. Only difference was that Dad and his friends all had Jamaican accents, which made *drankin'* and *smokin'* sound more like *dreekin'* and *shmookeen'*.

While I was picturing Snoop and his boys on a Friday night— and recollecting Dad and his boys last Friday night—the intro ended and I heard familiar sounds. It was "Gin and Juice," the song I knew. I had heard it on the radio and seen the video for it on MuchMusic. I tried to repeat some lines that I remembered as the track played, about him rollin' down the street with his mind on his money and his money on his mind. Snoop Doggy Dogg, man. He has a way with words, I thought. And it wasn't just the words: it was the beat, the way he *said* the words, the confidence he seemed to have, the vibe, the music. The soul. I pressed Stop on the booth deck. This was the cassette that I wanted. Snoop Doggy Dogg, man. I went looking for Mom.

"Can I get this one?" I asked, not even waiting for an answer. "Mom, this is the one I want. Snoop Doggy Dogg is the biggest rapper. He's from California. He's the coolest. This is what my friends are talking about. LeShawn has it. Joel has it. Please, Mom. Can I get this one, Mom? Please. Do you know who Snoop Doggy Dogg is? He's been on TV. Have you heard of him? Please, Mom."

"I've heard of him," Mom confirmed. "But are you sure you want to get this? It's filth, Matthew. You know that, right? I know who Snoopy Dogg is. I talked to your cousins, David and Jimmy."

I gripped Snoop's *Doggystyle* in my sweaty small hands. Handing it over to Mom this early in my plea could result in an easy loss, so I held on to it. I'd been handing over things in stores to Mom since I was six or seven, and almost every time either she ignored me while searching for the shelf I had found it on so she could return it to its rightful place or she looked away while telling *me* to put it back. When she was really tired, she'd rip the toy car or *Goosebumps* book or plastic action figure out of my hands and leave it on the nearest shelf, while explaining that we didn't have money for things that I wanted but didn't need.

"Do you know the difference between a want and a need, Matthew?" Mom would ask whenever a holiday rolled around. "We need to get toilet paper. We don't need to get you a new baseball glove."

Handing *Doggystyle* over to my mom was a no go for me. I was turning nine—almost a grown man. I would use my words. Especially because I didn't just want the album: I needed it.

"Mom, I know. It's filth, but it's music. It's just music. And I like it. I like how it sounds. Snoop Doggy Dogg is such a good rapper. Did you know he is from California?" Words. I knew I needed to use them. I knew I needed that tape.

"You sure you want *this* one? There are so many other really good ones in the store. What about Mariah Carey? You like when I play her in the house. I picked up this tape for you. It's called *Music Box*. She sings with such soul, Matthew."

"I know, Mom. She's good." I pressed the *Doggystyle* cassette into her palms. "But this is the tape I want. I need this, Mom."

Thinking about it now, I really don't know *what* my mom was thinking.

After the cashier rang us up, Mom handed me the plastic bag and told me that she wanted to stop in Canadian Tire before heading home. I usually hated going to stores like that with Mom—she scoured the aisles for literal hours looking for deals, and when she found one, she looked for the cleanest copy or the latest expiration date—but I would have stopped and started in a million stores for her because of what she let me pick out for my birthday in Sunrise Records. She hadn't bought anything for herself.

"We should get something for Daniel. It's your birthday, but he's only seven. We gotta make sure he isn't jealous. We'll get him something small," Mom explained. So we went to Canadian Tire and bought him a pack of marbles in a mesh bag on sale for $2, after she looked at eleven other bags first.

I got *Doggystyle* in the fall of 1994, almost a full year after it came out, and it was the first hip-hop album I ever owned. That's how Black culture came through Scarborough in the early '90s. Black movements and modalities came a bit late to us: brands to buy, ways to dress, slang to speak, music to listen to. I didn't even hear any of Tupac's music until after he died. Snoop Doggy Dogg was responsible for shifting my perspective on life. Tupac Shakur did too. As did a bunch of other Black men: Christopher Wallace, Shawn Carter, Nasir Jones, Curtis Jackson, Dwayne Carter, Jermaine Cole, Aubrey Graham, and Kendrick Lamar.

Since the day I took Snoop Doggy Dogg's debut album home, the hip-hop albums I've listened to have taught me more valuable life lessons and offered more insight into my world than any other education I have received. School taught me how to read and write, but hip-hop taught me how to articulate. I learned math from teachers, but from rappers, I learned how to calculate. My parents and my teachers and my neighbourhood told me that I should strive to "get ahead" in life. Despite conflicting ideas of what exactly "getting ahead" meant, hip-hop taught me about the life I was trying to get ahead in.

In some ways, hip-hop taught me *how* to live. When I heard Biggie rap about getting your neck slit quick if you talked slick around street niggas, I believed him. I watched my words around niggas who looked like they were real street. In high school, when Mr. Burke used a banana and a Trojan condom to teach us about safe sex, my boys and I laughed and cringed because we already knew the importance of condoms. TLC had shown us in their video for "Waterfalls" years earlier. Way before Mr. Burke rolled that slimy latex down the bottom end of a banana, most Black boys who were falling in love with hip-hop knew the importance of safe sex because we had watched a gaunt-faced man stare into his soul and at his reflection as T-Boz sang about those infamous three letters that took many to their final resting place. What I learned in class about succeeding in life was not quite as powerful as what hip-hop taught me about life itself.

Even though Jigga rapped with a smooth, arrogant cadence that bounced with any bass line, I knew that when he went on and on, song after song, about sex and murder and mayhem, his words were something for me to merely romanticize. Even though I wanted the money, cash, hoes, and all that, I knew they were not something to strive for. Jigga, like the rest of those men, rapped to us about things that they'd lived through. Boys like me didn't need to experience those same things because those men already had and then poetically explained them to us. Some, like Jigga, actually told us that by rapping about their life stories hopefully we wouldn't have to go through the same thing. Those men afforded us boys the opportunity to mimic without manifesting. Their lyrics allowed us to mime our way into manhood without maiming ourselves in the process.

Part of why I listened to that Snoop album over and over in 1994 and beyond was because Calvin Broadus seemed fictional to me. He loomed larger than life in his lyrics, interviews, and music videos— so real but make-believe at the same time. I could *feel* everything about him but couldn't quite *touch* his reality. I was a light-skinned kid from Canada; he was a brown-skinned man from California. He put cool words together like *gin* and *juice* and said cool things like *Gs up* and *hoes down*. I didn't know what that meant, but I knew that it was my type of cool. The girls at Golf Road Junior Public School picked between different spices to be cool: Sporty, Baby, or

Posh. Those girls at my elementary school adopted aspects of one particular cool, which was cool to all of them. But ultimately all of them girls were one type of spice—the white kind. And whether they wanted to admit it or not, most of the boys in my grades four, five, and six classes thought the Backstreet Boys were cool. And at times, I even wanted it that way. But to Black boys like me, LeShawn, and Joel, those boys weren't really cool cool. They weren't cool like Snoop was cool. And they definitely didn't have soul.

Still, though, we were not Snoop . . . yet. He was like our cool uncle. A cool character we could channel when needed. He wasn't exactly a role model, but he showed us a role we could someday see ourselves in because our skin more closely matched his than it did Nick Carter's or AJ McLean's. Snoop, and Black men like him, were the men we could watch and (try to) imitate. In 1994, Snoop was steering the vehicle of hip-hop, and we wanted in for the ride.

And the art form would take me for a trip.

The older I got and the more I listened to hip-hop, the more I knew how to analyze what was happening to Black boys like me. Sixteens detailed their grandiose victories and gave us lines for our small wins. Raps, as hyperbolic as they sometimes were, became less and less abstract in our childhood fantasy worlds. Over time, their stories told through rap and our lived realities blended parallel. As we got older, men like Snoop drew closer. The gap between us didn't seem that wide. The word *Illmatic* didn't make much sense to nine-year-old me when I saw it on the cover of a tape in 1994, but by 2001, Nas, draped in an orange velour suit and crouched down on the cover of *Stillmatic*, made all the sense. By the next year, we were all trying to live like our favourite Black artists.

In the late summer of 2001, while a lot of things were poppin', Mom took me back to the mall. Cash Money Records had come out and told us all that *we* were taking over for '99 and into the 2000s. In Scarborough, we still got things slow, but when we heard

Juvenile say those lyrics a year later, we felt it and ran with it. That summer, Mom and I were still willing to walk together—without holding hands—in order to get what we both wanted.

She wanted to bond; I wanted to stretch. She wanted to reach out; I wanted to pull away. Together, we walked to the bus that took us to the light rail transit at Kennedy Road, which then took us to the subway on Eglinton. From there, we took the Yonge line south to Queen. I was fifteen and had outgrown Sunrise Records and Cedarbrae Mall. She was fifty and knew way more things about life—and about me. Mom knew she didn't have to ask her white nephews what they thought about the latest rap album anymore. She had learned that if I wanted something, I would tell her myself. And she knew that I didn't want much, because I thought I was a man. And she and I were both figuring out what a man—and a Black man—meant.

She also knew that by grade ten, I was going to Cedarbrae Mall for lunch every day, despite the cheese and butter sandwiches she still packed me. She eventually stopped packing paper-bag lunches for me. At the time, I knew why she stopped, but I secretly still wanted those bland lunches she made. Despite everything sprouting up around me, I felt like she knew that I still considered myself a boy. And she also probably knew that I was becoming Blacker than she had ever envisioned. Despite me being half-white. Despite me being her child.

The mall entrance at the Queen subway stop was bigger than either of us had imagined. Mom hadn't been downtown to the Eaton Centre in years. The farthest mall me and my boys travelled to was a ten-minute trip west on the 54 Lawrence bus to Scarborough Town Centre. Being downtown in a massive mall with Mom was new, but we both knew what we had come for. The hip-hop cassette tapes she had bought me in the mid-'90s had evolved into these thin polycarbonate plastic discs. Discs that people like Tucker's older brother, Denver, bought and copied onto blank ones to sell. We no longer had to go to Sunrise Records to buy an album for twelve bucks; we just looked online at album covers after hearing a hot track or two on the radio, and then we'd ask Denver if he could burn a CD for us for $2. If Tucker and I stole enough blank CDs from Dollarama to give to Denver, he would burn our favourite albums for free.

I knew what hip-hop sounded like, and I had plenty of access to it at that point in my life. But by 2001, I also wanted to look like hip-hop.

I appeased Mom by looking for deals with her in Sears and The Bay. It was September, but Mom never missed an opportunity to buy things on sale that could be wrapped for relatives months later at Christmas. After a few hours of comparing ten versions of the same item, we finally hit up a few spots I wanted to check out. Foot Locker and Champs Sports were stores I could only dream about shopping in. We both looked around and decided that the Jordans were nice, but I could do with the $70 Nike Air Max low-cuts from the Bata store in Cedarbrae. We left those stores and eventually landed in a hip-hop clothing shop on the top floor of the mall.

I suggested a FUBU sweatshirt and some shiny black jeans with a label that read Enyce because Usher was on the brand's poster rocking a hoodie. I wanted to be like Usher. And Enyce looked and sounded Black—sounded and looked like some shit a nigga would wear.

Mom went to the cash register, bought the FUBU and the Enyce, and put the bag in my hands. We left the mall, and as we took the train back to Scarborough, I felt even more like a nigga. I couldn't wait to try my new clothes on while listening to Nas. And maybe a bit of Usher.

For Black boys like me, no aspect of culture shaped our identities, our attitudes, and our looks more than hip-hop. I wonder if white boys who went to high school in the '90s defined themselves by the music of NSYNC or Garth Brooks or Nirvana in the same way that we based our identities on a mosh pit of our favourite rappers. I knew the type of Black male I was engaging with based on who their favourite rappers were. I knew that a Nas fan was the typa nigga who carried himself in a serious manner and considered hood intelligence to be fundamental. A Jay-Z guy was interested in being the centre of attention and valued materialism above all else. Dudes who banged Tupac prized spontaneity. Our hip-hop stars defined our roles in life.

My favourite rappers' lyrics voiced my thoughts. Walking to school listening to the latest Nas or Jay-Z song on my Discman, I marvelled at how rappers seemingly saw parts of *my* life and put *my* experiences into a rhyme. These Black men, who made the music I nodded my head to, captured the echo that reverberated around me. They used words and aesthetics to produce vibrations that I couldn't shake, even if I wanted to.

When the musician's raps didn't connect directly with my life, I found other things to connect with. Their big successes were my small wins. The car they just copped was the new bike I saved up to buy in grade eight. My new FUBU sweater and Enyce jeans were their Gucci, their Louis, their Prada. They rapped about buying platinum jewellery; I bought cubic zirconia. And I swear you couldn't tell the difference in photographs. Their verbal and visual counsel taught me how to present myself so that the outside world viewed me how I hoped and dreamed they would. A Black boy who looked, walked, and talked the part. The part being the culture, which was so integral to so many of us that it was implanted in our souls.

These Black men talked to me through their verses; they were the older brothers I never had, giving me advice every time they spit over a beat. They were more than stars or heroes or role models to me. I wondered how they knew so much about me. I felt like I had a hand in writing their verses. They were me.

Kind of.

After listening to Jigga's *Vol. 2 . . . Hard Knock Life*, I didn't immediately rush out to become a crack dealer or some hardcore gangster in the hopes of taking the same path as Shawn Carter. But listening to that album, and others like it, did make buying that chocolate bar at the corner store beside LeShawn's house a little bit harder. I could just steal it. If I got caught, the shopkeeper wouldn't look at me any differently. That shopkeeper was sure that I, in my baggy jeans and Triple Five Soul T-shirt, was stealing anyway. Hip-hop helped me to define myself, but it also was interpreted by others to mean that we were all the same.

Adults weren't listening to "that filth" like we were, but they sure heard about it: famous young rap niggas were on television talking slang, waving money around, wearing baggy jeans, and not giving a fuck. Because we dressed like them but didn't have the millions of dollars or fame to ward off the condemnation that came with ascribing to the culture, we weren't given the same pardon society begrudgingly gave them. So young Black boys like me took the brunt of the backlash certain folks expressed toward hip-hop and rappers. My jeans were baggy, and I liked to wear fitted hats that matched my shoes; my imitation of rappers told people that I emulated them. Those rappers were me, but that didn't mean I was them. Outsiders couldn't see the difference.

I experienced this clearly late one night on a trip home during my first semester of college.

———

"Matthew, wake up. The cops are here," my mom whispered to me sometime after three in the morning. "Get up. Tiny's been arrested. Get outta bed."

My brother, Daniel, has always been big-boned. By the time he was ten years old, he weighed 155 pounds. My mother's brother, seeing me and Daniel standing side by side as children, gave us nicknames: I was Stretch, and he was Tiny. As I got older, my uncle's nickname for me fell away as it became clear that I would never grow into it. Daniel, however, didn't disappoint. He ballooned to 180 pounds, then 200, then 240, then 270 by the time he was a teenager. Even Mom called him Tiny.

"Alright, Mom. But why do I need to get outta bed just because *Tiny* got arrested?"

"I said the cops are here. You need to get up. They need to search the house, Matthew. Put some clothes on."

Tiny had gotten pulled over earlier in the night, and because they had found a gun on him, the police executed a search warrant on his home address—our home.

Tiny had always clung closer to the hip-hop music that glorified drug dealing, crime, and raw thuggish shit. By the end of grade nine, he was hanging around friends who smoked weed instead of going to class. After a few years, teachers didn't even have to downplay Tiny's presence in a classroom because he wasn't present at all—he had stopped going to school and started doing other things. Things that led cops to bang down my parents' front door at three a.m. and to serve my mom a warrant to search the premises.

I got out of bed and threw on a T-shirt and shorts. Sitting there, on the corner of my bed, I awaited instruction from four men who looked just like the dog catcher on the cover of the first album I had ever owned.

The cops told me to get up and move to the living room with Mom and Pops. We sat there while they hastily ripped through every kitchen cupboard, dining room cabinet, bedroom dresser, and hallway sideboard. After flipping over a few mattresses and not finding a thing anywhere, they moved to my bedroom in the basement.

"You can follow us down. Your room is downstairs, right?" one said, without making eye contact or even turning his body to acknowledge that he was talking to me. I nodded as I got up from the living room couch.

They rummaged through my closet. Unfolded my Enyce jeans and ripped my FUBU sweatshirt off its hanger, turning it inside out to check the seams. I sat there, kinda cold, a little bit diminished. Then they powered on my desktop computer, and while we waited for it to boot up, I thought about my brother and wondered how he felt. If he knew these cops were on the brink of stealing part of his life because of choices he felt compelled to make. If he knew how some of the choices he'd made of late were a direct result of the slimming possibilities he measured at sixteen or fourteen or twelve. I wondered if he knew that he'd long loomed older and bigger and Blacker than any of those choices. And that the relationship between choice and conscription was so thin for Black boys like us that the difference between stealing a candy bar or keeping a gun sometimes seemed irrelevant. Whether pocketing those M&M's or having a snub-nosed .38 tucked made any difference in the long run. Because the cops already believed it to be true based on what they saw when they looked at us.

The cops clicked open files and scrolled through pictures. Photos of me. Of my friends. Of my boys. Pics that looked like album covers. We were wearing oversized suits at my boy David's wedding.

There we were. Posing. All my boys and me. With our fingers stretched in front of the camera. Ring finger tucked, flanked by the thumb, with the index and middle finger spread while our pinky fingers stood tall, to root up a weird version of the number three.

Middle finger pinned by the thumb in another flick, left hand in the pocket, revealing another abnormal way of showing a three. Index and thumb cupped over each other to, yet again, demonstrate a weird collection of finger placements that coincidently showed another three. Justin Timberlake posed in pictures making a peace sign, while our rap and gangsta father figures and OGs on the block had cooler signs, especially on album covers. We imitated. Even when in rented-out, oversized suits for a brother who seemed too young to get married, we flipped our fingers in weird ways for a photo. They flipped the script when it came to who we could and couldn't be.

"Is this you?" a short, stocky, nerdy cop asked me while three of his colleagues continued scrolling through the computer I used for writing essays and watching porn.

"Huh, what? Me. Me?" I cleared my throat. "Yeah . . . yeah. That's me."

"What gang you in?" The way he asked was so nonchalant, so indifferent. He asked his question with such certainty that I had to beg his pardon. "MNL Boys? Bloods? Crips? What gang are you in?" He pronounced each word slowly while staring at me so hard it was like he was trying to burn holes in my skin with his eyes.

"You're joking, right?" I cocked my head sideways, hoping to avoid any shrapnel from his stare. "Nah. I'm not in a gang."

That cop took a small step toward me, closing the small space between my chest and his police vest. "Whaddaya call that?" He pointed to the computer monitor. To the photos of me and my boys happy, in shiny bronze vests, posing for the camera because one of our friends had just gotten married.

"What do I call what, Officer?" I knew what he was talking about, but I had also learned never to give police any more information than what was required. Hip-hop had taught me that.

The three other officers shifted their attention from digging through my jean pockets and shaking out my sweatshirts to me. Although I wasn't literally, I felt surrounded.

"You're throwing up gang signs in this picture here. Look at it." The mouthpiece with the blue vest and the stocky frame wasn't asking questions anymore. His words became facts. His partners didn't nod in agreement or parrot his sentiments. They simply fixed their gazes on me. More holes burning straight through my Black skin.

"Nah, those aren't gang signs, man," I said. "We're just posing for pictures. The pics look better like that. That's it. I don't know what else to tell you."

"No. These *are* gang signs, man. We work in the Guns and Gangs Unit. Who do you think you're talking to?"

These cops thought that because I was Black and lived in an area that didn't have the best reputation, that me posing in pictures with my fingers twisted out in front of my chest instead of buried in my pockets proved I was involved in gang activity. I'm sure they saw men who were in gangs pose in pictures the same way me and my boys did. Those men were probably influenced by the same music that influenced me. And the rappers who made that music were probably influenced by people in their own areas who were like those very men. We imitated the rappers. These cops couldn't see the difference. And because of that, these cops in my basement circling me couldn't see me.

"Listen, man. I go to college and play football. I'm here on winter break. I have a football scholarship and go to school down south," I said. "I'm a football player, not a gangbanger. I'm not into the same shit as my brother."

The stumpy mouthpiece didn't flinch. "What, you don't think so-called football players can be gangbangers? You play football in the States. Good for you, kid. That doesn't mean you still can't be involved in a gang."

He still couldn't see me; I knew that. But I wasn't ready for what came next.

"Take off your T-shirt. Put your arms out and turn around," he ordered.

I slowly did as I was told. I stood with my face to my bedroom door as the four of them examined my upper body. Now I felt the same size as the short, stocky, nerdy cop who was looking at my skin.

"Are you guys really checking out my tattoos?" I asked.

"Sure are," said the punk cop who seemed to have had a growth spurt in the last ten minutes. "Checking to see if any of them are gang-related."

I have a tattoo on my shoulder that reads *In God's Hands*. Another one down my left bicep says *Parkay*. Parkay was a margarine brand that ran a slew of commercials in the early 2000s with the tagline "Just like butter." When I started playing football, the star player on the team, Weezy, noticed me dropping a lot of passes and started calling me Parkay. It became my nickname.

Tatting my nickname down my bicep made absolute sense to me at eighteen. I loved every part of hip-hop culture, and one of those parts was the ink. I honoured hip-hop culture by imitating it—all my boys did—so I had those two tattoos. It's what hip-hop did for me. The police stood around me while forcing off my shirt so that they could take a closer look. That's what hip-hop did for them.

From grade four to university, hip-hop showed me how to be, how to exist in my body, and how to articulate myself as a Black boy. In one instant that was all snatched away, leaving me feeling like a nigga on the auction block. A body to be sold off because of everything that had been sold to me.

I stood there. Felt them watch me. Silently studying me. Passively revelling in their power over my body. I hadn't done anything to merit this naked appraisal other than posing for a few pictures that resembled the album covers I cherished and having Black skin. It didn't matter what I said or did. It didn't matter that I went to college and played football and liked hip-hop because it was part of my culture. Those cops never saw me.

The cops eventually left, having found nothing that would further incriminate my brother, and leaving my parents and me in a home that took weeks to put back together.

It seems to me that hip-hop was just another fancy tool we used to try to take our shackles off, but all it actually did was reconfigure the chains still fastened onto us. It seemed as if hip-hop's entry into mainstream culture signalled the arrival of Black abundance, Black creativity, and acceptance of Black life. A vehicle made for us by us that could drive us toward belonging. Instead, racism, once again, stick-shifted that machine off the highway toward Black acceptance.

Hip-hop's gradual mainstream welcome felt nothing like the wave of Black collective upheaval Malcolm and Martin inspired during the civil rights movement in the '60s. Hip-hop's brand of sonic and aesthetic culture splashed louder and harder than the Black Panthers' roars did in the '70s. Our new music lifted Black culture to heights that even Magic and Michael couldn't reach while playing ball in the '80s and early '90s.

But because of its force, the world outside hip-hop doubled down on its stance and pushed back on us. Thanks to Tipper Gore and C. Delores Tucker, U.S. Congress slapped Parental Advisory labels on albums deemed explicit. Mainstream journalists rallied against the vile degradation, bad reputations, and proclivity to violence said to be reinforced through our art. Judicial courts across both the United States and Canada sought to establish links between rap lines and real crimes. The clothes and slang and tattoos and mischief Black boys like me carried out became symbolic of all that was "wrong" with our culture. I was whittled down to my baggy jeans and my cocky gait. Because I espoused an aesthetic that showed me how I could exist as myself, I became a thug, a gangster, a criminal. We thought hip-hop gave us a seat at the table, only to realize that it has always been a game of musical chairs.

Those cops in my home that night probably didn't listen to hip-hop music. And if they did, they definitely didn't relate to it the way I did. They saw it as if they were looking through a two-way mirror at thugs, gangsters, and criminals, always on the other side. They told me to strip because I'd contorted my fingers like Nas and Lil Wayne did. They saw a Black kid with tattoos and equated me to images of Tupac with a shaved head, bandana on, and *Thug Life* written across his stomach. But the hip-hop they peeked at through that glass was a mirror for us. I packaged myself in a certain way because I saw myself reflected when I listened to my favourite rappers. The world outside hip-hop viewed me as just another piece of that package.

I still wonder if any other form of music has played such a potent role in classifying a body the way hip-hop has for Black males. Did Oasis, House of Pain, Nirvana, Nine Inch Nails, Green Day, Alanis Morissette, or the Tragically Hip do for my white brothers what hip-hop did for my Black brothers? Did they use that music to soothe pain and to forge their identities the same way we used our music for healing and consoling? When they listened to Blink-182, Limp Bizkit, Coldplay, U2, Weezer, and the Smashing Pumpkins, did they notice similarities, common experiences, and mirroring values like we did when we heard Mobb Deep rap bars about war going on outside and the shook ones who were scared to look?

Did the mirror that music provided us look back at my white brothers and tell them, the same way Jay-Z told us, that regardless of what type of nigga we existed as—light skinned, dark skinned, rich or poor—we were all still niggas.

Did they feel their music the same way we felt ours? Or were there other mirrors that they could see themselves reflected in and grow? On TV, I saw white newsmen telling positive stories about other white men. Most of the movies and TV shows I watched with Mom starred white people in white situations in all-white worlds. When I woke up in the morning and walked to school, my teachers told us that we could be anything, but none of them looked like me. Their words couldn't penetrate the psyches of me and other Black boys not only because they didn't look like us but also because they failed to show us tangible evidence that we needed in order to believe. So, we turned a deaf ear to their talk. Our ears were only attuned to stories we heard through rhythms on wax. We paid attention to what hip-hop told us. It was the only real thing we had.

It was probably the only thing those talented Black men, who wrote songs the whole world sang, had as well. Or at least the only thing those Black men thought they had. Even capitalizing on their talents was minimizing. They told us that. Jay-Z once rapped about rhyming with more conscience content, like Talib Kweli, if that sold more records. Kweli was a brilliant, obscure New York rapper whose songs were about Black liberation and the complexities of being a Black man in America. Jay-Z's rise to fame came through hit songs like "Money, Cash, Hoes" and "Big Pimpin'." Both men were articulate; both men were brilliant. I was a young Black boy when I became a heavy Jay-Z fan. I heard a few of Kweli's records in high school, but I was inundated with the messages Jay-Z had been sharing since I was in middle school. He was Hova—a literal rap god. And his songs were everywhere: on the radio, on MuchMusic, on *Rap City*, on BET, on the loudspeakers in Foot Locker and Champs Sports in the mall. And it was his message, his vocals, that landed over and over in our ears. The gatekeepers—the ones who let things through and held things back—made sure of it.

The Jay-Z song with the line about how his lyrics would be different if thoughtful modalities of Black intersectionality were accepted is called "Moment of Clarity." The song was released well after Jigga had been cemented as a hip-hop icon. It was one part of a fourteen-song set titled *The Black Album*, the title an ode to the Beatles' famous *White Album*. In November of my grade twelve year, I listened to *The Black Album* with the same fervour that I imagine white teenagers listened to the *White Album* back in November of '68.

On *The Black Album*, when Jay-Z rapped about doing it for the money I was ready to listen. When he claimed that no one in rap was as good as he was for as long as he was, I felt it. When he declared how he was both hood and pop, equally hot and strong, I felt him. I felt our way of making music. That song was titled "What More Can I Say?" I knew men like Jay-Z were just making music, telling us about things we seldom saw but knew existed. I knew my life went on beyond their sounds and songs. I loved it but, to me, it was just music. Songs to sing along to. Just some good ol' "Ob-La-Di, Ob-La-Da" to listen to.

But the gatekeepers showed those brilliant Black creatives like Jay-Z otherwise—and we came to live that otherwise too. The reflections after Biggie Smalls's and Tupac's deaths made the art of hip-hop music all too real. It made those cops in my home that night—and people more powerful than them—open and close the gates for Black boys' creativity, inspiration, and reflection. The only rappers elevated by the gatekeepers were those who exposed partial truths about living while Black. All for their profit. Our come-up as a culture through hip-hop still managed to stifle Black boys like me.

Since my mom bought me Snoop Dogg's *Doggystyle* in 1994, hip-hop has changed a lot. I went from listening to rappers tell tales about selling drugs to tales about promethazine, codeine, and

Percocet. Back then, Tupac's *Thug Life* stomach tattoo tipped off the cops to tell me to take my shirt off while my mom and dad were sitting upstairs in zip cuffs. Today cops probably wouldn't ask me to strip because most new rappers have tattoos on their faces.

If I were growing up now and listening to today's hip-hop music, I'd have tattoos beside my eyebrows instead of on my arms and shoulders. Maybe there'd be no need for those cops to see more of my skin while executing their search warrant. But they'd still look at a young Black man like me the same way: from the house side, behind that white gate.

Rap artists and geniuses doubled as reporters for and from the hood. The problem has always been with teasing the messenger from the message. Our messengers told parts of our truths. Because they kind of had to. Today it's harder to find the truth in the music. It's harder to *feel* it. Because it's even bigger than it was when I walked into Sunrise Records in the summer of '94 and begged my mom to buy me a tape titled *Doggystyle* by a cartoonish, genius Black rapper named Snoop Doggy Dogg. Because the outside world has gotten inside this thing of ours. And our mirror is all fucked up now.

I still don't know what Mom was thinking in getting that tape for me. I wonder if she didn't force my nine-year-old Black hand into hers as we walked to Cedarbrae Mall to pick out my birthday present because she was realizing that her whiteness could no longer protect me from my Blackness. That one of her parental powers was being a gatekeeper for her children. Part of being a gatekeeper is opening gates when they need to be opened, not just when the gatekeeper benefits from their opening. She understood that so many other gates would be closed by more powerful gatekeepers simply because of the colour of my skin. And that the white-picket-fence life she grew up aspiring to was as make-believe as the Black life Snoop Doggy Dogg rapped about. It was real but fake at the same time. That really it was just music after all. Maybe getting me *Doggystyle* for my ninth birthday was her way of letting me know that she would be okay with the things I would be forced to learn, to grow up with, to strive for. These aspirations would be different from hers because, despite being half-white, I was Black. I would learn and feel differently than she did. My mom might have known that the hip-hop music I would grow up listening to and the hip-hop culture I would learn to imitate were something I would call my own. For better or worse.

THE BALL DON'T LIE

"You could get hurt. It's so violent," she said. "Plus you're really good at baseball. Why don't you just keep playing that?"

My mom's concerns for my safety weren't the only reason she wanted me to play another season at shortstop for the West Hill Yankees instead of trying out for a position on the Scarborough Thunder football team. The West Hill Baseball League grand-fathered in their $60 summer membership for families who re-enrolled year after year. A season of peewee football would cost her $150, plus tax. Paying $90 more for me to play a different game didn't make sense financially. We still made cheese sandwiches out of the loaf ends and went without shampoo and snack foods until they went on sale.

"Mom, I don't like baseball anymore," I said. "The Blue Jays haven't won since '92. We're in the damn 2000s. Nobody really cares about baseball around here anymore. I'm gonna be good at football." I willed my words to express my full intentions to her. I knew that feelings and meanings were two of the more pressing things she still paid attention to. "I promise, Mom." Willing words, not empty ones.

"Oh, I don't know. Ask your dad." Ever since I stopped holding her hand on walks to and from stores, Mom's belief that her advice impacted me, as my independence expanded, seemed to be weak-ening. "You're good at baseball, Matt. What's the difference?"

Pops didn't really care which sport I played anymore. He started not caring about anything I did by the time I was thirteen. When I was seven or eight, he seemed fully invested in watching me and Tiny compete in sports against other boys our age. Back then, if I bothered him enough, he would play catch with me in the backyard for thirty minutes before telling me that he needed to start barbecuing. He was one of the parents who coached our community league teams, sitting with other dads during pre-season meetings, setting up the game schedules, and shouting basic instructional platitudes like "Play hard!" and "Let's go!" and "Keep your eyes on the ball!" from the dugout during games.

By the time I decided that I wanted to be the next Barry Sanders instead of the next Barry Bonds, he'd found another passion too. He'd gradually resigned from his coaching obligations and slipped into the crowd of fathers who hung out in the parking lots during our little league games, sipping from cans in brown paper bags while pungent clouds of weed smoke lingered above them.

I couldn't blame either of my parents for their hesitancy when I told them I wanted to play another sport at age thirteen. My over-the-top dreams of becoming a professional athlete collided with their daily grind, their reality of mediocrity. The promises I made to myself were the stuff of childhood fantasy compared to their squabbles about the car insurance going up after Pops got pulled over midday with a beer in his lap, or the inordinately expensive phone bill because calls home to Jamaica during the week were more expensive than on weekends. But signing me up for another year of sports was less trouble than making false promises to visit Niagara Falls or Disneyland.

"If you want to play football, find out when the registration is and go sign up, Matthew." Dad had a way of making the complicated simple. Especially after a few bottles of Beck's and some Appleton. "We'll figure out how to pay for it once we figure it out."

"Cool. I'll find out and let you know. Thanks, Pops." He didn't respond. He was eating his dinner on the couch in the living room, watching the Leafs game with his eyes closed. It looked like he was savouring every bite.

The number I picked for my first football jersey was 30, the number of my favourite player at the time, Terrell Davis, who played running back for the NFL's Denver Broncos. I grew to adore him when his team won back-to-back Super Bowls in '98 and '99. Mom surprised me on my fourteenth birthday with a blue and orange Broncos jersey, the name *Davis* in ironed-on white letters across the back. A big white *30*, outlined in orange, was painted on the front and back of the nylon knit. I kept meticulous care of that jersey. Wearing it felt like becoming a part of him; owning it kind of felt like I owned a part of him.

I even wore it to my first football practice after Dad got the $150 together for me to play. Putting on that jersey helped me identify with Davis. I practised and played and watched football that whole summer and again that fall, becoming obsessed with it. I didn't yet understand that by wearing Davis's jersey while watching him run for touchdowns on television, I was consuming both the figure of him as a Black man and the implicit racism that was being marketed and sold to me. Instead, I bought more jerseys: Deion Sanders's Cowboys jersey because he was Prime Time; Barry Larkin because he was my favourite baseball player—plus the Cincinnati Reds had the illest-looking grey, red, and white colourway; Tracy McGrady because every boy in Toronto seemed to own one; and Michael Wiley because he was my favourite player at my favourite college, Ohio State University. All the jerseys I owned represented who I wanted to become: a professional athlete. A professional football player.

A professional athlete seemed like the ultimate job any Black boy like me could aspire toward at that age, both realistic and lucrative. Winning races with schoolmates at recess and earning first-place ribbons at track meets came with congratulatory messages from teachers and other adults; slowly over time, those achievements outweighed any acknowledgment I received for answering questions correctly in class or putting together solid projects for the science fair. The passive messaging I received told me that physical gifts were more important than intellectual ones for Black boys like me. An imagined career path in sports was made more plausible by the articulated imaginations adults bestowed upon my own body.

Driving a truck for a living like my dad or working a trade like most of his friends paid the bills but left little money for anything else. The career path to becoming a lawyer, or a doctor or CEO, seemed more fictional than accessible. The first time I saw a real Black lawyer was on TV when I was around ten years old. He was representing a former football legend charged with murdering his wife, but he talked like a character in an NBC melodrama. Not for me. Plus no one pushed me to pursue those paths anyway. Becoming a professional football player felt within reach—like a dream that I could eventually obtain.

Those jerseys made my dream more real. Those jerseys were something I could touch, something I could feel. My boys and I owned jerseys like we once owned toys. Those toys back then, like the jerseys we now donned, were objects that fulfilled our desires to be like someone else while remaining ourselves. Objects under our control at all times and not shared. Objects we collected and poured our dreams into as we gradually absorbed the idea that ownership was a zero-sum game. We eventually believed that almost all things were meant to be owned. Everything from materials to merchandise to mentality to men.

When Toronto birthed its NBA franchise, the Raptors, Black boys like me watched Damon Stoudamire and Marcus Camby vie for wins against our favourite basketball stars. Concrete courts and basketball hoops sprouted up around Toronto, and boys flocked to them, trying to be the next Allen Iverson or Penny Hardaway. When I went over to the courts behind the 399 Markham Road apartments with Tucker and the rest of my boys to run a three-on-three match or some full-court action, I learned a new phrase: ball don't lie. The phrase became so prominent in the basketball lexicon that we even heard it uttered between NBA players during games.

The first time I heard some older kid yell "Ball don't lie" at another kid, I was confused. Of course the ball doesn't lie, I thought. How could it? It's round, made of leather, and weighs less than a premature baby—how could such a thing lie? When shot at the basketball rim, it either went in or it didn't. But the first time I heard that older kid yell "Ball don't lie" as he shoved it back into that other kid's chest, I learned that the rules for pickup games were different from NBA ones. When someone claims they've been fouled while trying to score, they get the ball back. Whether they deserve it or not. Because the sport, as an institution and as an idea, is based on black and white rules. Based on merit. When the person who claims the foul gets the ball from his opponent—because that's how the unwritten rules of basketball go—the opponent gives in because that "ball don't lie." Sports are a meritocracy based on action, not falsities or myth. That ball is supposed to represent truth. So, shoot it again, liar. It's going to rim out and you're going to miss your next shot because, as they say, ball don't lie.

After my first year on the Scarborough Thunder peewee team, I showed enough drive in my new sport that Mom and Dad scrambled together $150 for me to play another season. I changed my number to 21. I thought that by wearing 21, I would embody one of my favourites, Deion Sanders. I trained and practised and felt

I was moving along a pathway that would allow me to excel while staying true to myself.

I was getting better at the craft of football and could tell by my results on the field. Coach Bubba gave me more playing time and worked with me after practice on fine-tuning my skills. "Morris, I think you can have a future in football if you keep working like you've been working," he told me on a late August afternoon days before the Thunder's first game of that season. "You played running back last year, but if I'm being honest with you, running backs are a dime a dozen. If you switch to defence, you can be special. I can see you playing defensive back at the next level, for real. You remind me of Mundle and Roberts."

I knew of both guys. They were older boys from Scarborough who went on to play football in college and the CFL. Guys I could relate more closely to. "Think about switching positions. And pour your all into it. You have the intangibles. Trust me."

His words gave me more confidence, which allowed me to look at myself differently. I was becoming Matthew, the athlete, the guy who is good at football. My confidence helped me look at opponents on game days as if they were meagre. The more meagre they looked to me, the better I performed. The better I performed, the closer the parallels I drew between me and the athletes I admired. The self-fulfilling prophecy carried on. That ball wasn't lying.

My parents ponied up the increased price of $180 for me to play the following year. My brother and I enjoyed fewer Jos Louis cakes and Passion Flakies for a few months. I changed my number again, this time to 5, because by then playing football in college seemed like a viable option, and that was the number I swore I would wear once I made it to Ohio State. Just like their star player Michael Wiley, just like his jersey that I owned.

Cabbage rolls, potatoes, and whatever meat Dad took off the barbecue filled me up by seventeen, a senior in high school. I was a football player—one of the better ones in the city—with the potential to capitalize on my physical assets. Wearing number 5 for Ohio State University, which only recruited the best of the best, seemed a bit far-fetched at that point. But, somehow to me, making it to the NFL didn't.

After five years of playing football, I had managed to pull myself up by the bootstraps. By my last year of club football, my parents didn't have to pay the registration fee because it was waived. Scoring touchdown after touchdown in my senior season at Cedarbrae, I began to seriously believe in the American dream. The male teachers at school talked to me more about my performance in games than my performance on their tests and assignments, and I took their pushing me toward athletics as a good thing. It felt like they cared about who I was. They showed me that the ball—regardless of the sport—didn't fib to those who used it well.

Five years before they anesthetized my body to scrape away scar tissue and displaced bone fragments from my shoulder joint, I was running onto the field at the SkyDome, ready to compete for the Greater Toronto Area high school football title. Seven pounds lighter than the weight I hoped to be when I became a professional, I took my position as quarterback and prepared for our first play. I no longer got nervous before games. The practice I had put in over the previous years was paying off; scoring touchdowns on offence and making interceptions on defence was something I expected to do multiple times in the sixty minutes of competition. Reading my last name in the sports section of the *Toronto Star* and the *Toronto Sun* during grade twelve math class made my dream more real.

It would be my last high school football game, win or lose. I still hadn't earned a college football scholarship, but that wasn't a thought in my head seven minutes into the first quarter. I was focused on lifting my team out of the early 14–0 hole we'd fallen into. Northern Secondary School's star player, Matt Black, zoomed past our defence for two quick scores. We hadn't lost a game all season: my teammates and I were facing failure for the first time.

At halftime, we were trailing Northern 21–8. I had scored one touchdown in the first half but had been pressing too hard, trying to prove how much better I was than everyone else on the field. Northern had anticipated I'd do this, and I fell right into their trap. They stymied my efforts every time I tried to make a big play.

Before the second half started, I stared up at the roof of the SkyDome, stunned by its vastness. I was dreaming that maybe one day I would be back playing under this roof as a Toronto Argonaut. Or a pro on another CFL team. I was hoping that Coach Kim's halftime adjustments would work and we would win.

"Offence! Meeting over here," Coach Kim yelled from the corner of the locker room. We gathered around him. "Their outside linebacker, number 45, he's the weak link on their defence. He can't read our outside option play. Morris, we're going with a no huddle offence all second half. Get the boys lined up, and whatever side number 45 lines up on, that's where we're running. Can you handle that?"

"Yes, Coach," I answered.

Northern's 21–8 lead closed to 21–15 after I handed off the ball to my boy Ishamar and watched him rip a forty-yard touchdown run late in the third quarter. Our defence shed their first-half jitters and instinctively knew that we needed to swarm Northern's star Matt Black any time it looked like he was about to touch the football. Fortunately, Northern didn't look to feed him too often in the third quarter. Then, in the middle of the fourth, I scrambled on a naked bootleg, looking for a teammate in the end zone to pass to. I trusted my legs more than my arm and decided to tuck the football and run for the score. I needed the second touchdown almost as much as I needed us to win that game. I trotted across the goal line and put my team up by one. Northern 21, Cedarbrae 22. We added a field goal to extend our small lead with under five minutes left in the game. Northern 21, Cedarbrae 25.

When I looked up at the scoreboard clock reading 00:00 and heard the referee blow his final whistle to signal the game's end, I ran in erratic ovals and fell to the ground in the middle of the field. And screamed as loud as I could.

I had fully invested in the self-fulfilling prophecies that Black boys like me receive from schools, society, and sports. I was saturated with the idea that local Black sports stars were destined to fulfill their dreams and identities by virtue of their bodies. That fucking ball, man. It told no tales.

The hot air in the warehouse smelled like WD-40 and cardboard. Samaco Trading Limited was a housewares distribution company, and Dad worked as one of their truck drivers. When Tiny and I were younger, we spent summer days riding in the truck cabin beside Dad. We rode up and down Highway 401, stopping at different giftware, glassware, and home decor stores, watching our father deliver skids full of product. We had the most fun when he let us ride back in the cargo area of the truck after his last delivery of the day.

That summer, before I left to play football and go to school at Western Reserve Academy in Ohio, both me and Tiny were old enough for Samaco to hire us. The $6.80 an hour was better than begging Mom for a twenty every week or so, and warehouse work didn't seem that bad or hard—at first. Label, stack, and pack boxes onto skids, then shrink-wrap them when the pallet gets to about five feet. Repeat. Until break time, or lunch, or the end of the day. Stand at a station along the conveyor belt, squeeze the spring-loaded scissors on the packing-peanut dispenser until enough little pieces of Styrofoam densely cover the products inside the box, seal and tape, and send the box down the line. Repeat. Until break time, or lunch, or the end of the day. Unload box after box out of a forty-eight-foot semi-trailer. Repeat. Until break time, or lunch, or the end of the day. At the end of the day, I blew my nose until my snot was no longer black.

During break time, or lunch, or at the end of the day, most of the workers would gather outside. Buying items off the food truck and smoking cigarettes, small groups would assemble all over the back parking lot of the warehouse. Guyanese and Trinidadian women hung out on picnic tables adjacent to the back doors. Indian men sat together in the grass near the edge of the lot. Tiny and I stayed by our dad, who lingered with his friends around the back of the food truck, talking shit about order mix-ups while sneaking gulps of beer and brandy from their cars. Dad and his work friends belonged to a group too—men from Somalia, Jamaica, and West Africa. Men with calloused hands and deteriorating lower backs. Men who used their bodies to put food on their families' tables.

Because my body had earned me recognition on the football field and in newspapers earlier that school year, I was invited to the owner's office a few times that summer. Andy was a well-liked man. He held annual company parties at his mansion in the Bridle Path. He was a University of Toronto alumni who'd played Varsity Blues football.

We talked in his office because he wanted me to consider playing football at the University of Toronto instead of going down south. Walking from the dark, dusty warehouse floor in the back into the bright, spacious management offices in the front was like stepping between two different worlds.

The front offices smelled like cool conditioned air mixed with lime-scented Windex and fresh paper. As in the back parking lot, small groups of people gathered in the front offices. Delicate white women with lightly blushed rose quartz faces answered phones and typed on keyboards with their cottony fingers. Clean white men with sharp jawlines and sharper handshakes gathered inside glass-walled offices behind doors that said Sales or Operations.

The walk through the front to Andy's corner office was no longer than forty yards. In that space, I saw completely different bodies from the ones in the warehouse. These bodies in the front, I could tell, weren't using their hands to put food on their families' tables.

Even though I could see this distinction, at eighteen I couldn't have cared less. I couldn't see my own future in the breaking-down bodies of my dad and his co-workers. Mine was strong. Sharp. Intentionally calloused for me to profit off *correctly*, in the way that I was told to. Watching Dad driving around, sweating to unload Andy's product for $8.50 an hour, served more as a cautionary tale than a road map for me. It was a warning that I should use the next few years to take advantage of my own body before it was used up or started working against me.

That summer in the back of the Samaco warehouse taught me that I should continue to optimize my strength and sweat for a dream, not an hourly wage. That spring, coaches from Western Reserve Academy had kept their shoes on in Mom's living room while offering me a scholarship to come play a year of prep school football. That was a warning, too, but one that I ignored.

The dream was still touchable when I earned a football scholarship to Colgate University in upstate New York. Colgate football wasn't anything close to a big-time, blue-blood football program like Ohio State, but it was a shot. It was a scholarship to play NCAA football. I could still play well, get drafted to the NFL, sign a multi-million-dollar contract, win a Super Bowl, maybe even be named MVP if I played really well that day, and retire close to my fortieth birthday. That was my dream. That was the goal. All I had to do was train really hard and play really well. The rest would sort itself out. That ball told me so, and it never pump faked.

Days into my freshman season at Colgate, I tore my shoulder, but I didn't know it. I had known something was a bit off during that last year of high school. The summer after my senior year, I felt a slight discomfort one afternoon while training. I chalked it up to the bumps and bruises of practice. Although the injury subsided for months at a time, it never fully went away. Minor contact would bring the pain back. My arm would pop in and out of its shoulder socket while I slept. When it started to happen during pre-season training camp at Colgate, I told team doctors that it felt as if my arm was on fire. I couldn't even raise it up until they massaged the two bones of my AC joint back into place. The next time it occurred, they fitted me with a shoulder brace and told me to hop back onto the field when I was ready. Once the burning subsided, I was ready. Always. I had to be. My body was my investment in my dream. *The dream. I built it so. I couldn't let my body sell me out.

I didn't get any playing time during my freshman year, despite getting the jersey number I had asked for during the recruitment process. I asked my coaches for the opportunity to compete. Injuries made it easier for them to tell me that the players I'd become boys with were better. So, from the sidelines, I watched my boys win some games and lose others. I still owned my jersey number, 5. My coaches still owned me.

After another year of putting my body through the rigours of practice and preparation without much playing time, I left Colgate. I knew that I would never be a student without the athlete part. Even thinking about being a regular college student there merely for the books and bachelor's degree stabbed at my self-confidence.

Sports was something that I couldn't live without. Abandoning that part of my identity would mean I'd have to foster an entirely new persona—one I had never met and certainly wasn't yet prepared to meet. Their sports programs and my Black identity were so intertwined that it was impossible for me to relinquish any part of either one.

I'd mulled it over with a few friends until one of my boys, Matt Black, who was playing Division II football at Saginaw Valley State University in Michigan, put me in touch with his head coach. One forty-minute phone call later, I was offered a scholarship. By late January, I was unpacking my duffle bags in a second-floor duplex I shared with three other guys on the football team. We'd never met, but we shared the same dream.

Weeks into spring practice at Saginaw, I knew my shoulder was torn. It kept popping out while I slept, and it would dislocate while I warmed up for practice. My coaches finally scheduled an MRI.

"You know how the bottom of a frayed pair of jeans looks?" the orthopaedic surgeon asked as I sat down in his office for my post-examination appointment. "That's what the tear in your shoulder labrum looks like. Ripped to shreds. So you have two options. You could quit football, start rehab and physical therapy, and in a decade or so when you become a father and your kid wants to throw a baseball around the backyard with you, you'll be able to."

"Uh-huh," I said. "And the second option?"

"We can proceed with surgery on your labrum. With rehabilitation, you could potentially play football again in anywhere between twelve and eighteen weeks. But I wouldn't recommend it. The playing football part." His medical advice burned hotter than all the times my shoulder had dislocated. "Totally up to you."

I looked at the assistant coach who had driven me to my appointment. "Up to you, Morris. This is your life." It was indeed my life. But he was my coach, and football was my game. I felt indebted to both. The game, I thought, would realize all the dreams I had for myself. That ball had given me something to believe in.

"When is the earliest I can get the surgery?" I asked.

Thirteen months after they anesthetized my body and gave me a six-week-long prescription for Percocet because my body was "too young, athletic, and muscular" to need the typical eight-to-ten-week post-surgery prescription, I was walking to my team's sideline, dripping sweat in the middle of the University of Toronto's season opener against Waterloo. Months prior, I had transferred back to the university my dad's boss, Andy, had wanted me to attend.

I had just returned a kickoff thirty-two yards. Above average for a return, I thought. Enough for me to put on a highlight reel, I thought. Enough to keep alive my teenage dream of looking up toward the ceiling of the SkyDome while playing for my hometown team, the Toronto Argonauts, I thought.

During the last play, I thought I found a gap, a small crack in Waterloo's defence. A path to the end zone. After digging my left foot into the ground to pivot and taking quick strides, I thought I was off to score. On the fifth step, my right shoulder, arm, rib cage, and skull violently struck an opponent I didn't even see. Mom had always been right: I could and did get hurt. My helmeted head was the first part of my body to hit the turf. All of a sudden, I couldn't think. My brain, like a television being unplugged, turned off.

When it turned back on, I was walking off the field with an assistant coach and a medical trainer. It felt like a rerun. Something I had watched before. Like that time in Ohio when I didn't know what had happened seconds after having collided with another player and couldn't say what day it was or what country I was in. This time, I held onto the memory.

I followed the trainer's medical penlight with both eyes and answered her questions. I knew what day it was and what team I played for. How could I forget? I had spent years sweating, trying to get to this point.

"Morris, you just got rocked. But you almost broke it, man. You alright?" my assistant coach asked.

"I know, Coach. I thought the same thing," I answered.

"Your eyes are lookin' kinda glazed. We're up on defence in a play. You good to go in?"

"Man, that hit was soft. C'mon. I'm good, Coach. Built for this."

"Good. Here's your helmet, son. Let's go."

Minutes later, I did break it. I returned the next kickoff ninety-seven yards before getting tripped up on Waterloo's one-yard line. The play helped turn the game in our favour, and we won. My last name was in the newspaper the next day. I felt close to making it again. Definitely not the NFL, but maybe a few years in the CFL. Reaching for a deferred dream still felt like reality that last year of college. It had to be. It's what that ball had long been offering me.

Outside sports, what could I do with my life?

I'd been trying to pull myself up by the bootstraps for over fourteen years. I'd been trying to perform a seemingly impossible task—to succeed as a Black boy—through one of the only avenues I believed were open to me. I fixed my identity to being an athlete, because it made me feel safe. I bought into the arresting notions that confined my body to baseball diamonds, basketball courts, and football fields.

And I was one of the lucky ones. Although sports damaged my body, it didn't completely mutilate it or the self-image I had underneath Morris the Athlete. On the surface, I thought I was exceptional. That I was different. That I was more like Deion Sanders and Terrell Davis than the Black boys who settled for being their fans. My brain bullied my body into believing that matter could in fact rule over mind. Into buying my own local-sports-star hype that necessitated my muscles to grow stronger through bench presses and sprints and sweats. I believed that sports was the only way I could be exceptional.

I was limited without realizing it. I pushed relentlessly to be an athlete because nothing and no one else invited me to explore different options. Even while my body tore at its seams, I thought it was the only thing I had to propel myself forward in life. That Black abundance told Black boys like me that our exceptionality was found in our high calves, wide pecs, and sturdy shoulder blades.

Six years after they anesthetized my body and planted plastic anchors into my shoulder bone to thread the muscles and tissues and ligaments back together, I was seven pounds over my ideal playing weight and preparing for the Super Bowl.

My childhood team, the Denver Broncos, was playing the Seattle Seahawks. My idol, Terrell Davis, had retired twelve years earlier. That blue, orange, and white jersey Mom had bought me when I was fourteen still hung in my bedroom closet at my parents' home. I hadn't worn it in years, but we didn't throw things out.

I brought two bags of tortilla chips and one bottle of rye over to Ahad's condo. It had been three years since I'd played real football, and Ahad had been on the team I'd last played for. We'd become boys through our shared dream about what the sport and our bodies could provide for us, through the myth that sports stations sold: that the only thing Black boys needed to do was pull themselves up by the bootstraps. For weeks leading up to that Super Bowl, we listened to stories about the Seattle Seahawks star defensive back, Richard Sherman, and his rags-to-riches triumph to live the American dream.

Sherman grew up in California, coming up out the mud and bricks of Compton. His standout high school football resumé earned him a scholarship to college. He performed well enough to get drafted into the NFL and was now on the brink of super-stardom. His story was almost mine. And the stories about Sherman that permeated sports media leading up to the Super Bowl focused on his fine-tuned athleticism, his brash personality, and his *unique* intelligence.

Sherman was smart enough to get into Stanford University, an institution known for its elite academic standards. The media played this up. He was a lesson for Black youngsters looking to make it out of their dire circumstances. He was a young Black boy who beat the odds and proved that abundance was available to kids like him as long as they worked hard. The story told about him suggested if you shot the ball the right way and practised enough, things would touch twine rather than rim out.

But beneath the messaging around Richard Sherman and his rise to success was a white lie of meritocracy. A white lie that says we Black boys can become what we hope and dream if we work hard at it—without mentioning that we can only hope and dream of certain things. A white lie that says because Deion Sanders and Terrell Davis did it, you can too. A white lie that uses sports as a foundation for the good ol' "hard work pays off" myth without mentioning that we have to work twice as hard as our white counterparts, still to this day.

That myth that meritocracy prevails across racial boundaries is bounced around, spun, and tossed to the point that all Black boys believe they can use their bodies to succeed in life just because some other Black boys were able to. It's the white lie that had us in the parks telling each other, "The ball don't lie," when almost everything else around it does. But Richard Sherman wasn't to blame for it. Neither was I. Nor were my parents for letting me play foot-ball. The lie is to blame for how limited its truths are.

And even though the ball doesn't lie to Black boys when we use it to play, in the end, the *game* still controls who wins and loses.

Me and my boys watched that Super Bowl at Ahad's crib while sipping ryes and sharing stories of our football lives. We rooted for players to make plays and swore at the television when they did things we didn't like. We all accepted it when the Seahawks gained an early lead and never looked back.

Then we talked about why that team had won. That's what the team with the better players is supposed to do. We believed that things ought to be decided by merit. Sports taught us that. Unfortunately sports is one of the only institutions where that myth is usually true. And even then, Dad still needed to figure out a way to get that $150 for me to play in the first place.

While watching more than twenty Black men give their blood, sweat, and bones in order to win, we didn't talk about the limiting ways Black boys are allowed to proceed in order to succeed. Or why so few Black men outside sports and entertainment are publicly lauded for their successes.

We watched the twenty or so Black men fight, scrap, and collide, trying to salvage parts of their bodies for the big houses, fancy cars, and stocked fridges we once dreamed of. Watching the game unfold, we didn't talk about the managers, executives, members of the sales and operations departments, or owners who put just as much (or more) food on their families' tables without risking their brains, bones, and skin in order to do so. Instead we watched and thought about buying a Richard Sherman jersey the next time we were in a mall. In the hope that by buying into parts of him, we could salvage parts of us.

———

Eleven years after they anesthetized my body and reattached my shoulder in its proper position, I was sitting in my parents' basement, twenty-one pounds heavier than my playing weight, watching my Toronto Raptors vie for their first NBA championship against the Golden State Warriors. The Raptors were trying to cap off a historic run after trading for NBA superstar Kawhi Leonard in the off-season. I was chasing double shots of Canadian Club with ginger ale when Raptors point guard, Kyle Lowry, dove into the front row trying to save a loose ball. He couldn't save the ball, and he stumbled into opposing fans, losing possession for his team.

Instead of jogging back into position, Lowry stood over two $3,000 courtside seats and a fan who was sitting in one of them. Lowry brusquely signalled for a referee to come over. I put my drink down. I couldn't understand why a simple loose ball was taking so long.

The television replay showed the fan shoving Lowry after he had fallen onto those courtside seats and shouting at the Raptors point guard. Lowry seemed furious. The referees huddled up and deliberated. Minutes later, the fan was escorted out by stadium security. The game continued; I poured another drink.

The next day, after trudging through a cloudy Thursday where my class of twenty-three seemed more like sixty-six, I drove to the gym to sweat out the rest of the rye that clogged my belly and brain. I still needed workouts to fill a part of my day, no longer fuelled by the burning desire to excel at the craft I loved but to burn off the calories I'd consumed while watching the athletes I once felt so close to. I plugged my earphones into the treadmill and flipped through the stations until I hit TSN.

The time I spend on the treadmill always passes quicker when I catch some highlights of recent games or previews of upcoming ones. Listening to sports commentators argue back and forth about the series made the post-workout jog less dull. What I heard for that thirty minutes, however, were not predictions about the next games but grown men's thoughts about five seconds of the game I'd watched the night before. I found out that the name of the man who shoved Kyle Lowry was Mark Stevens.

They weren't really talking about the game. Over and over, they replayed the short clip—of this Mark Stevens shoving Lowry after he stumbled into him and repeatedly telling him to "go fuck himself"—that ironically didn't even happen between the lines of the actual basketball court. While sweating on that machine, I learned who Mark Stevens was.

Stevens was not merely a rich fan who paid over $3,000 to be entertained on a Wednesday night. He was also a so-called self-made billionaire and part owner of the Golden State Warriors. The talking heads gabbed back and forth about the NBA levying its punishment onto Stevens—a $500,000 fine and a one-year ban from attending any Warrior games.

Some considered the punishment too harsh, declaring Stevens a man who got so caught up in rooting for his team that when an opposing player toppled into him, he felt like he was part of the action. Others saw the consequences as inadequate, saying that Stevens's behaviour demonstrated the abuses of entitlement, that he felt like he owned a piece of Lowry. They eventually got back around to talking about that ball—that unassuming, unassailable, bouncing leather object. But without diving into how it can become the cause of crossed lines between who we are and how we identify. Fan, performer, owner, player, the body, the brain. Lines that some of us cannot cross. They kept their commentary underneath the canopy of how that ball never lies to us.

I drove home, my head whirling with contradicting thoughts. Thinking about who deserved what. How privilege allowed some people to demand that sports be merely a service. How the men who possess the skills to play the game had to bargain with men who possess the actual game itself. How all those jerseys I owned felt like one thing to boys like me and probably another thing entirely to boys like Mark Stevens. And how, after the age of ten, boys like Mark Stevens probably didn't take too seriously the idea of buying into players' bodies for the sake of their hopes and dreams. Instead, those boys probably bought into the idea that they could enjoy, be entertained by, and possibly even own other bodies one day. And if they followed the path trod by others who looked like *them*, their dreams would come true too. After all, that had to be what the ball told them.

Nearly a decade after they anesthetized my body and worked on fixing the rips inside me, San Francisco 49ers quarterback Colin Kaepernick took a knee and was subsequently blackballed from the NFL. Video after video had surfaced of Black men getting shot by officers of the law, so, as a form of protest, Kaepernick decided to kneel when the American national anthem was played before 49ers football games. He used his fame and platform to shed light on the Black people who were buried after bullets from police guns tore through them and on the excessive force cops used against Black bodies, killing them. I watched five-second clips on my phone of men running and getting shot down, simply because they ran. Or resisted. Or sat in their cars. Trying to escape. Just like me. Hoping to make it. Just like me.

Just like most of my boys, I fell short of my American dream. The life I hoped for rimmed out. I bought a Colin Kaepernick jersey after he took a knee to stand up for people who looked like us. By name, Colin Kaepernick sounds white. He sounds like a blue-eyed, blond-haired German guy. I don't know what the NFL would have done if Colin Kaepernick had been white.

I know what sports did to my body. Over the years, it bent some parts out of shape. It dislocated, strained, and sprained other parts.

But it also created muscles that became shields. It calloused parts of my skin so that it could endure certain pressures. It reconfigured parts of my mind so that I was able to perform rigorous exercises. Exercises that required belief, determination, and dexterity. It showed me that the ball didn't really, truly lie. It allowed me to dream. It gave me hope.

I was fortunate that Mom allowed me to play football and that Dad found the cash that afforded me the opportunity. I didn't end up walking onto that SkyDome field wearing a professional jersey with one of the many numbers I had owned, trying to imitate one of the many bodies I had learned to become. But I did earn a college degree because of the ball. I also used my experiences in sport to answer job interview questions that eventually got me hired. Jobs outside sports. Jobs that didn't require me to use my hands to put food on my own table. Jobs that demanded more of my heart and my mind.

I don't know what would have become of me if I hadn't tried to make it in football. I don't know if I would have gone to college. Honestly. Or how I would have approached high school if I hadn't been pursuing a college athletic scholarship, which required a decent GPA and SAT score. Or how I would have used my body in other potentially more dangerous ways, if others hadn't encouraged me to use it for sports. The ball helped me grow into myself. Even though after I was done playing, I was relieved to reclaim my own bones.

Yet it still irks me when I watch a sea of Black on professional courts and fields, and only a sprinkling of men with the same skin tone watching from management purviews. All those Black men who put their bodies on the line for that bottom line. They do make millions, but they do so in a profiteering industry rooted in the buying and selling of their bodies and images. All those identities. All those pictures. All that manual labour they provide for the companies they work for. Just like my dad and his friends did at the Samaco warehouse: they were akin to the Black men I looked up to in those jerseys, playing sports to win games, earn trophies, and sell tickets. Seeing and dreaming of both types of labour split me in half.

I can't stop visualizing the density of Black men who work in those warehouses compared to the almost exclusive whiteness of the men who own and operate them. The proportions are strikingly similar to those of professional sports teams: Black men labour on the courts and fields, and white men own the teams and leagues. Manual labour and sports. Every time I turn on a game and forget about rooting for my favourite player, I remember how similar sports and manual labour have always been. How one type of body is always ginning up for the sake of another's entertainment and profit.

To distract myself, I cloak myself in yet another jersey. Something I can own. Something that reminds me of the dream I once had. Something that makes it a little easier to believe in the myth. Even when some parts of it seem true, others feel like white lies. I still don't know if the ball ever lied to anyone else.

THE FRESH PRINCE SYNDROME

The University of Toronto was my third college in three years. And the whole college thing was wearing thin on me. I'd had enough alcohol, parties, sex, hangovers, fights, classes, courses, and exams at the first two colleges to make me walk that elusive straight and narrow path at the third one. I didn't even plan on making new friends there. Get in, get the grade, graduate, get out. That was the goal—no fucking frills whatsoever.

It was my first time in school in Toronto in over five years. After graduating from Cedarbrae Collegiate, I spent a year at a prep school in Ohio, two at Colgate University in upstate New York, and another one at Saginaw Valley State in Michigan. I came back to Toronto from the States with a certain self-assured air when I met other Black students. Black students who lived on hip-hop and were from broke and broken parts of the city like me. Now I had a one-up on them. At least that's how I felt. I had lived in the Black Canadian's contemporary motherland and experienced the mecca of hip-hop and Black culture. To most Black Canadian kids born in the '80s and early '90s, the United States of America was the shit. But the fact that I had been there and done that was small consolation for finishing my college career a mere forty-five-minute subway ride from where I started my elementary one.

The classes were familiar. From the professors who stood at the front of Romanesque lecture halls and expounded on slide after slide to the students who took notes and pictures of those slides while scrolling Facebook. The seminar classes—with fewer students and a lot more participation—I enjoyed the most. Not only because I found it easy to bullshit my way to at least an A minus without doing much of the required reading but also because I could make my presence known in other ways.

By the third week of the first semester, I was good. I no longer had any problem finding all the buildings and houses and halls where my classes were held. I'd even made a few friends and done some of those other things I thought I'd had enough of. Comfortable in my new setting, I slipped back into my persona. And those seminar classes were the perfect stage for me.

That same week, I walked into class later than usual. Except this time it wasn't on purpose. On the steps up to the second floor of Northrop Frye Hall, I'd run into Mahmoud, a brother I had gone to high school with. I was fucking shocked; I had no clue he was in school. Despite seeing him with a backpack full of books and shit, I couldn't believe that he had made it to university. In high school, he was a grade below me. He was one of those Black boys I played sports with after school or saw hanging out at the Burger King at lunchtime. I didn't know know him, but he seemed like all the other niggas who went to Cedarbrae.

We talked, then wrapped up our conversation by exchanging numbers. I continued to class, stopping when I finally got to the door. I checked my Casio G-Shock: twenty minutes late. Shit. That was pushing it, even for me. But I was fully committed to my persona.

Before entering the classroom, I pulled back the Lil Wayne song I was listening to on my iPod and turned the volume up slightly. I took one earphone out just in case I needed to hear any immediate shouting in my direction from the professor. Although I could hear Lil Wayne's screaming claims of being a millionaire who was tougher than Nigerian hair blasting from my earphones, the wooden floor creaked even louder as I walked toward an open seat at the back of the class. I didn't miss a beat; I strutted with confidence. Still in character. I waited.

I took my backpack off my shoulder and let it hit the ground. And waited. I took the other earphone out. The music sounded like it was coming from a mini speaker, competing with the professor's lecture for anyone within a ten-foot vicinity. I slowly lowered the volume on my iPod, looked up at the professor and around at the students, and then turned it off completely. And waited.

It was a history course called France since 1830. I wondered why college courses broke up the history of a country into so many different time periods. The professor was going on about the Dreyfus affair. Apparently it was some big scandal in France back in the day involving treason and espionage. The professor didn't skip a beat either, continuing on about antisemitism and a great miscarriage of justice. I wondered why he kept on lecturing as I came in with music blasting, pants sagging, hat on, and bag thumping on the ground. I wondered why he continued speaking without saying a word to me. And the other students? I got nothing from them either. No smirks or winks of appreciation. No silent congratulations. No telepathic Yes, Matthew! Fuck this dude talking this boring-ass shit in this boring-ass, pretentious-as-fuck classroom. Let them know who you are! Play that Weezy louder.

Nothing. No one in that room cared.

I don't know when this started, or stopped, happening. Did it stop when I came back to finish my undergrad degree in Toronto? Or had I never noticed that my performance was gradually losing its appeal after the miles I had spent bending my Blackness down in Ohio or over in Saginaw or way back upstate New York? I only noticed how that lack of response affected me as I sat in that class-room. And after that, everything I knew about moving through hallways and classrooms was in question. The school felt like a foreign land that I no longer knew how to navigate. My compass no longer worked. All because no one took notice of me when I walked into that college classroom late.

I held on to one thing: my performance hadn't been lost on any-one when I was in high school.

Cedarbrae Collegiate Institute in Scarborough wasn't some specialized high school for theatrical performance, but it sure did create a lot of actors. And I was one of them. We weren't the kind of actors who left for Hollywood; we were the ones who stayed in Scarborough and had big roles in our own recurring dramas.

Weeks into grade nine, I walked to the parking lot facing the school's automotive tech shop and saw that the cheap chain lock I used to secure my bike was sliced in half, dangling on the railing. My bike was gone. A few days later, I watched as a grade twelve boy walked my blue CCM through one of the halls on the first floor that led to the exit where all the smokers hung out. There was noth-ing I could say or do. He was closer to a man than a boy with his filled-out frame and goatee. I didn't even have peach fuzz above my lip or in my armpits yet. I felt less than. Maybe even invisible. It was my first lesson on "knowing your role" in high school.

I adjusted quickly. I'd already picked up on a few things in mid-dle school thanks to teachers like Mr. Turner. Things like how the world teachers inhabit rarely resembles the reality of students like me. In Miss Ross's grade nine English class, I learned that my opin-ions of *To Kill a Mockingbird* were only acknowledged if they fell in line with hers. If I had a different take on *A Midsummer Night's Dream*, she was quick to point out that I didn't quite get it, that I needed to try harder.

Over time it made me feel invisible in the classroom. My thoughts and ideas didn't matter. My experience was treated as irrelevant. Grades nine and ten felt portentous—a dress rehearsal for how things would play out in the real world. At the time, I didn't understand why I felt so distant from the values that high school teachers extolled in their lessons, or have the words to explain it. All I knew was how I felt. And I felt like saying, "Fuck it. School don't like me and I don't like school much neither." School wanted to play with me, mess with my head.

As my body matured and hair started to grow in places that signalled my coming into manhood, me and my friends replaced the big kids who smoked at the exits of first-floor hallways, starred on sports teams, and stole bikes from grade nine boys. We had studied and accepted our new leading roles. Not just from the older kids who fucked with us during our grade nine and ten years, but from everything else we watched outside school.

The summer heading into grade eleven, I spent most of my time with Tucker and a few of our other boys playing basketball behind his apartment building. We'd get together in the early afternoon, walk over to the court behind 399 Markham Road, and wait until we could put together a team that could run off a few wins in a row. Our lungs and backs never gave out on us, so we'd be there for hours. When we were satisfied and ready to move on to something else, we would ride our sometimes-stolen bikes over to my house. My home always had a little more food than anybody else's. And as long as my mom wasn't home, we could fill up on bagels, cookies, and juice without worry. With snacks in hand, Tucker and I, and whoever else made the trip over, would find a spot on a couch in my living room. We usually spent those summer afternoons washing down our food and drinks with episodes of *The Fresh Prince of Bel-Air*.

Will Smith's character hooked Black boys like us. In *The Fresh Prince*, Will had nothing, but he possessed so much of what we wanted. I gravitated to his backstory. He came from West Philadelphia, where he'd spent most of his days chillin' out, relaxing, acting all cool. Just like us. After school, he'd play basketball outside with his boys. Just like us. He got in one fight too many, so his mom became worried about his future. By grade eleven, my boys and I had all been suspended from school at least once. We'd all had "the talk" with our moms about "staying out of trouble" and "growing up" and becoming *good* Black men. We would nod our heads, and our moms would shake theirs. The intro to *The Fresh Prince* alone hooked Tucker and me and the rest of my boys because we felt like we were watching ourselves on the television screen. The fact that our parents didn't understand hadn't even hit our radars yet.

Will moved to sunny California to live with his rich uncle Phil and was exposed to a whole new world. I watched as he became the star basketball player at Bel-Air Academy, and I hoped that I could do the same thing on the football field at Cedarbrae Collegiate. I learned how to make an impression on girls in my school from Will who picked up girls with lines like, "Hold up, baby. See, I noticed you noticing me. So, I just wanted to put you on notice that I noticed you too."

Smooth.

When Will acted out in class at Bel-Air Academy, I figured out that the class clown—not the studious nerd—gained the most attention. When I saw Will turn that navy-blue blazer inside out to show that pretty paisley print on the lining, I grasped how my sense of style could come from being unique, individual, and loud. Through that show, I learned how to turn parts of my insides out.

Black guys like me, coming of age in the '90s, were inspired by Michael Jordan, Mike Tyson, and Michael Jackson because they were Black and had *made it*. Rappers were our idols. But I never grew to be six foot six, didn't have a ferocious left hook, and could only moonwalk in socks on linoleum floors. I liked freestyling but had never seen any Canadians really do it as a legitimate career.

For Black boys like me, in high school back then, there was no more aspirational figure than Will Smith in *The Fresh Prince of Bel-Air*. He was a reflection of us—a mirror reflecting our reality back to us. I tried my best to soak up Will's lessons and hoped they would direct me through English, math, and science at Cedarbrae.

At the start of grade eleven, when I should have been putting my best foot forward, I walked with an exaggerated and confident gait. I stepped into first period English class late every day. My teacher— let's call her Ms. Schulze—didn't say anything to me the first few times. She just stared into my eyes with a look of blistering confrontation that revealed how much she was holding back. Though she never said the words, it felt to me like she was holding back her desire to scream, "Why the fuck are you coming late to my class, on purpose, with a smirk on your face, you ungrateful nigger?" She thought that because my reading of *Othello* was incorrect to *her*, that I couldn't read other things, like her contempt for me, with crystal-clear vision. She didn't know that I could feel her eyes screaming from behind her glasses. I usually responded by chuckling with my friends who dapped me up as I found a seat in the back. My defence: I was developing my character; I was trying on a persona. Will in *The Fresh Prince* taught me that I could do that. I was acting in a movie and I was the main character.

By grade eleven, I cared about getting high marks, but I cared about performing more. In class, I would occasionally answer a question or two posed by the teacher, and I was getting good grades on the tests I completed. When we took tests, I used that time to bring out the Carlton Banks inside me. I was still a little nerdy. I was the Black kid who, when I wasn't with my friends, read the required textbook pages and completed the assigned homework. Every now and then, my boys would ask, "Yo, how did you know the answer to that shit Ms. Schulze was asking?"

"Man, they was talking about that same shit in a movie I watched last night. Samuel L. Jackson was going on about some Shakespeare shit at the beginning of the flick. I didn't get to see the end though. Amanda was over. N'ah mean?"

I was lying.

"Yeah, she's a freak!" Greg was lying too. We both knew it, but we were both so good at acting by grade eleven, so good at cheating on ourselves for the sake of the feelings girls trusted us with, that we kept up the charade. All of my boys did. Because we believed in the distorted constructions of Black masculinity that swirled around us. We were flipping our insides out while keeping hard truths folded in.

"Yeah, son. I got lucky last night and lucky in class today. Your boy on fire!" Somehow, slandering girls diverted us from looking at the ugliness of our insides. "Let's go hoop. My crib or Tucker's spot at 399? It's nice out. Probably nuff people ballin' right now."

"Let's go to the apartments. Last time we went over to your place, your mom went ballistic on us over the bagels. I ain't tryna catch that fire today," Tucker joked.

Our mouths and our words bent our Black bodies out of harm's way. We scripted ourselves away from real talk. Lost was a deeper and more honest conversation about intelligence, work ethic, and pretending to be something else for the sake of our insecurities. We all stuck to our scripts. We left to play ball, subconsciously vowing to keep honouring our roles at school.

Our teachers played their roles too. They executive-produced the endings of many episodes we starred in. My tardy appearances to Ms. Schulze's class became too much for her to accept. "You're late, Matthew," she would begin. "This is the third time this week."

"Yo, my bad, Ms. Schulze. My bad. Got caught up in the hallways today. Lost track of time. My bad."

"'My bad'?" Ms. Schulze repeated incredulously. "'My *bad*'? You come into an English class, late, saying '*my bad*'? Just find a seat."

"Sorry. I'm sorry, yo," I responded, waiting for a reproach for my continual use of *yo*.

I had an answer for her if she continued to pursue the script. I was ready to follow her "And don't refer to me as *yo*" with a casual response like, "Yo, my bad, Miss. My bad." She didn't bite. She just stared at me.

The more I learned how to perform as the main character in my classes, the more teachers like Ms. Schulze noticed, attempted to correct me, and surveilled my actions. I desired attention, like every other teenager. But in grades nine and ten, when I was myself, when I expressed an opinion, I had been made to feel invisible. Only my persona got attention. Midway through grade eleven, I learned that I got noticed among the sea of Black and Brown faces by making a splash around authority figures and cannonballing into deep waters, instead of gliding smoothly through those waves. Fuck Pamela Anderson and David Hasselhoff—we weren't trying to signal we needed saving *Baywatch*-style; we weren't even willing to save ourselves. And teachers like Ms. Schulze seemed to only throw their Kisbee rings in after we were already deeply submerged. So we used Will Smith, *Fresh Prince*-style, for the wins.

By the end of grade eleven, I still hadn't come ashore. Saturated in the identity that comforted me the most, I came to class later and later, walked in listening to music louder and louder, and traded barbs with teachers every chance I saw fit.

If Ms. Schulze didn't bite, I knew how to bait her. If she said nothing when I arrived late and sat at the back near one of my Black friends, I would start a conversation with him that was just loud enough to interrupt whatever learning was taking place. Sometimes she would stop what she was doing and stare at me until I got her message and stopped talking. I stopped talking, but my provocation had been successful. That meant I won.

Sometimes she would attempt to discipline me with sarcasm, with rhetorical questions designed to get under my skin. It didn't work. The costume and mask that I wore were becoming more and more like armour. My persona was fully developed and impervious to her contempt. I won again.

On rare occasions, she'd summon all of her educator's authority and press the buzzer on the classroom wall. "Matthew! I've had it with you! Take your stuff and get out. To the principal's office, right now!" She didn't seem to realize that by kicking me out of her class, she was ceding her authority over me. Whatever happened in the office—whether they called my parents, kept me there for the rest of the day, or suspended me—I would eventually go back to Ms. Schulze's class. And when I did, I could claim the final victory.

I needed that win for me and my boys because we were losing in other ways. The lessons our teachers taught us were fairly simple to digest. It was what they didn't teach explicitly that was tough to swallow. That in order to be successful you needed to think like them. In order to be valuable in their eyes, you had to not only understand but also value their culture. Our school taught us implicitly that venerating white culture was the only path to success. The omission and suppression of Blackness from our learning environment seemed to be more explicitly taught. It was an overarching, long-term tutorial designed to teach us that Black culture wasn't relevant to success at all. These were lessons that only Black boys like me had to learn. White teachers like Ms. Schulze forced their world onto us and acted like we had nothing to bring from our world into theirs. As if we were bare and empty, coming inside from the wilderness. As if the purpose of our classrooms was for us to soak up everything about them and then spit up what they offered us. Only to be empty again. To remain silent. Invisible. Unless we were willing to change. I realized that anything I said *would* be used against me. And that I could only speak if I was ready and willing to plead to their charges.

Our right to an unbiased education was denied. So we adapted, like we've always done. We doubled down on our roles instead of conforming. The muzzle they placed on the real me forced my persona to get loud in other ways.

It hurt me to change, but I wasn't left with many options. Wanting to do well but acting like I didn't care took a toll. Rejecting labels placed on my Black body made me weak. By grade eleven, I was diving for cover. I was learning what I could from school, then going home to watch *The Fresh Prince* with my boys on my couch, guarded against revealing any psychological deformities.

In one episode, Will's boy from his old West Philadelphia block, Ice Tray, comes to visit him at his posh new residence in Bel-Air. When Will introduces Ice Tray to his cousin, Carlton remarks, "So you're also a disadvantaged youth, I hear?"

After pausing and staring back at Carlton, Ice Tray asks Will, "Hey, man, what's up with him?"

"It's a tan," Will responds.

Me and my boys sat in my living room after playing basketball on a hot summer day and laughed with the television. We were Ice Tray. We were Will. We laughed at Carlton. And at Black guys like him that we knew, nerds who sucked up to teachers. Black guys who stabbed at our unfortunate circumstances as if we had a choice.

The Carltons seemed to me no different than the Mr. Turners who told us to pull up our pants, or the Ms. Schulzes who said that our way of expressing Black abundance was worthless. That our way of pulling up to class and engaging with school was obscene. That the ways we existed as students was unartful. The disrespect. We never wanted to be Mr. Turner or Ms. Schulze because we valued our Black identity even if they didn't. We also didn't want to be Carlton because of his psychological proximity to people like Mr. Turner and Ms. Schulze. We refused to digest the white righteousness that led to our culturally sanctioned self-loathing. We drew closer to Will's ways and his adaptability, his capacity to become the Fresh Prince of Bel-Air. We continued watching the show. Our show. The show that showed us who we were.

"Yo, what up on the schoolyard, huh?" Will asks Ice Tray.

"Ah, school, man. I don't bother it, and it don't bother me," Ice Tray answers.

Another laugh track played, but I sat silently on my couch with a bagel and cream cheese—the plain kind, because we hadn't learned about herb and garlic yet. Ice Tray's words echoed in my brain: "School, man. I don't bother it, and it don't bother me." Damn, Ice Tray. How did he know exactly how I felt? I mean, Ice Tray knew.

"Education *is* the mortar that builds the temple of success," Carlton says.

He was right. But at sixteen, I agreed more with Ice Tray's response than with Carlton's fake-ass platitude.

"Like, who cares?" Ice Tray says. Another laugh track told me that the audience agreed. It told me that they sided with Ice Tray too. It was okay for me to keep playing, keep clowning, keep resisting.

After a commercial break, Ice Tray is alone with Will reminiscing about good ol' times back in Philly.

"Same old Prince, man," Ice Tray begins. "You know, when I first met you, you was carrying your books in a pizza box so that nobody knew you were studying."

"Yeah, that was cool till them guys jumped me tryna steal my pizza. They was upppset," Will jokes.

The laugh track played again. A little longer this time. We laughed too.

Me and my boys didn't hold any long or deep or truthful conversations about anything other than Mase's new *Harlem World* album or whether Kobe could ever be better than Jordan. We didn't need to talk about anything deeper than rap or sports. We didn't talk about the episode we just watched other than the funny parts. "Yo, school don't bother me, and I don't bother it," Tucker said after Greg asked if anyone knew what was going to be on the science test he had in a few days. I knew what was going to be on it; the science teacher had told us. But I didn't feel like turning all of my insides out. That would be dangerous. We already had a place to express how we felt: school.

I never needed to carry my books home in a pizza box like Will did, but I certainly hid my academic inclinations from my boys in other ways. And when I was questioned about my motives, because Will had laughed it off, so did I. Being vulnerable about pursuing academic excellence wasn't an option for the Black teenaged boy on TV in Bel-Air, so who was I to champion that on my own in Scarborough? I wished that Ice Tray had ended that scene by telling Will that it was okay. That he didn't need to hide parts of himself. That he could turn all of his insides out and maybe that would make his outside feel better too. But he didn't. He just laughed at his joke and kept it moving. I got why the Ice Trays of the world didn't go deeper into those things with guys like Will. They were hiding too.

By the end of grade eleven, coming to class late and sitting at the back had become as much a part of my school-day routine as brushing my teeth in the morning. I had also picked up some other characteristics to cement my Blackness at school. Acting abrasively toward authority figures in trivial moments was compounded by my nonchalance during more consequential encounters. I wore my hat in class despite the no-headgear policy. I kept it on until they told me to take it off. I did this period after period, day after day. I had become a walking contradiction—a living, breathing oxymoron. I perfected my act so well that, over time, it became natural. My act was no longer just that.

I found out how well my character had been received in English class that May. Those tit-for-tat spats I had had with Ms. Schulze had festered into a growing animosity between us. We were so deep in our roles that she no longer kicked me out of class when I was disruptive, and she barely said a word to me when my lates piled up day after day. At times, we simply locked eyes. Scrimmages invisible to everyone but us.

For the final assignment, we had to write an analysis of Nathaniel Hawthorne's *The Scarlet Letter*. We had one hour to compose an essay that explained the significance of the book's title. Despite hiding it from my classmates, I actually enjoyed the book and had kept up with Ms. Schulze's daily reading requirements. I saw a bit of myself in Hester Prynne. I felt that the labels placed on niggas like me were bullshit and hypocritical. But I never cared to explain these things during class discussions. That would have been some Carlton Banks shit.

I pored over my essay—watching the time, reading over what I had written, looking at other kids in the class while wondering what they were writing down, and wondering what Ms. Schulze would think of my final piece.

The more I got into the essay, the more upset I became. I didn't know why I was getting frustrated. Was it because every time I looked at the clock it seemed like it was lying to me? Or because every time I turned in an essay to Ms. Schulze, no matter how big or small an effort I put into it, I received the same grade—a C minus? Perhaps my agitation stemmed from how they did Hester Prynne so dirty—and some teachers, Ms. Schulze especially, didn't see how they were doing the same thing to Black boys like me. Maybe I wasn't a walking contradiction after all. Maybe *they* were the oxy-fucking-morons. And fucking hypocrites.

I tried to regain my focus on the significance of the scarlet letter. I had filled out three-quarters of a page. Definitely not enough for a grade eleven final essay, I thought. I had to get to a page and a half. That would be sufficient. That would be acceptable. But I felt myself running out of words because I'd gotten carried away thinking about how bad Hester Prynne must have felt on a daily basis because of a label she had to wear forever. I was sixteen, and I had a label I'd be wearing in perpetuity too. My mind wandered off again: I became immersed in how fucked up it was that my Blackness was also a scarlet *A*. So I decided that I would see how much of a label I had finally become.

"You and I both know you're not even going to read this. I can write whatever the hell I want on here, and I'll still get the same grade."

Two sentences. I wrote them near the bottom of the page, flipped it over, and kept writing. Back to *The Scarlet Letter* and its seminal significance. I got to my quota—a page and a half—and I flipped my essay back over to make sure my name and the date were at the top. I waited for the period to end.

The next few times I went to Ms. Schulze's class were nerve-racking. I actually started coming on time, scared that this last attempt to provoke had taken things a little too far. I contemplated asking Ms. Schulze if I could talk to her after class and apologize for my mistake. I wanted to tell her that it had been a long year, and that I was sorry, and that I was exhausted, and that it was difficult being a young Black kid at a school like Cedarbrae, and that she didn't understand how much my need for attention played into my persona, and that it was indeed a persona and not my true true personality, and that maybe some of it was my fault. I wanted to tell her that I was actually smart and wanted to do well, but I didn't know how to show it in class without losing the identity that I needed to hold on to so badly, and that I didn't know how to negotiate with my Blackness and be kind to myself because I was afraid that I would become Carlton Banks if I did so, and that I really wanted to be the Fresh Prince instead.

I wanted to tell her that it didn't seem safe to turn all of my insides out, so I just showed the pretty paisley parts, the parts that I thought were pretty enough for other people to like. I wanted to tell her that for Black boys like me, sometimes the parts that we showed were actually the ugly parts, because it was an ugly world and being ugly back was sometimes the only way to survive, especially when you were scared and scarred. And that coming late to class was just an act—a performance, a part of my persona, something that I had developed but was also encouraged to develop by teachers like her. Not only by my teachers but by the world around me—and we all know how important that is and what it teaches us about us and what it renders useless. I acted the way I did because I felt neglected and thought that attention was better than invisibility.

But I didn't ask her if I could talk and she could listen. All of that was just too heavy to let out. So I waited.

I didn't even want to look at my essay when Ms. Schulze handed it back. I searched her face for a sign of what I was in for. She revealed nothing. She explained to the class how our essay grades would be weighed in our final course marks.

A few students shyly asked questions about rewriting the paper on the same topic with more time or on a book we had studied over the semester that they were more familiar with. She bluntly answered "no" to those requests and began going over the details of the final exam. As she talked, I mustered up the courage to look at my paper. I noticed red ink throughout my paragraphs: the misuse of a semicolon in one spot, circled sentences with "verb-tense agreement" written in another. I zoomed in on the bottom of that first page, where I had written those two sentences: "You and I both know you're not even going to read this. I can write whatever the hell I want on here, and I'll still get the same grade."

Nothing.

No red ink circling those sentences, underlining. No comments in the margin.

Ms. Schulze dismissed us before the bell rang. I was frozen in my chair, thinking that perhaps now she would say, "Matthew, I need to speak with you for a moment." I kept glancing at her as I packed my bookbag and walked toward the door. Nothing. She didn't even blink in my direction.

I met up with my boys at our lockers shortly after. "Yo, how'd you do on that essay you was talking about the other day?" Tucker asked. "You got it back, right?"

"A fucking 62, bro," I vented. "C fucking minus . . . again." I was stunned for a second, and I didn't know what to think or what to say to my boys. "And you wanna know the worst part?" I said, shaking off my vulnerability. I was ready to get back into character.

That day in English class taught me that I could never win the game by playing it the way I had been. The character I developed and played from late in grade nine until the end of grade eleven festered in me until I could no longer tell if I was imitating the art I saw on *The Fresh Prince* or if what I saw was a reflection of the true me. If it was not truly me, then I was addicted to my performance. The wound that Ms. Schulze and I opened up inside me— culminating in me ignoring her rules for writing an essay and her ignoring my rules for reading one—could not be closed.

During my last year of high school, I knew that grades would be important, but it was also important to enjoy the last months of my youth: listening to hip-hop music, dating girls, and playing sports. I still came to class late and sat in the back. I still had to be told to turn off my music and take off my hat. I still didn't open my mouth when teachers asked questions. The occasional times I did, I still didn't put my hand up and was reminded by teachers to do so if I wanted to speak. I looked for every opportunity to resist school in the most passive and petty ways. I did these things because school still rejected me, and I really needed it not to.

In grade twelve, those school books came home with me every night—not in a pizza box but in my backpack. Despite the dark depictions of my neighbourhood, the Scarborough I lived in wasn't as bad as the West Philadelphia Will described. The threats to my body for attempting to attain academic excellence weren't as acute. But when Black boys who looked like me discovered that some other Black boys tried to earn decent grades by behaving in ways that the school deemed decent, they made subtle remarks that made us feel less Black. That's where all this started.

I repeated those remarks to other Black boys. We all skirted the truth, careful not to step on it. School taught us that. When I was caught in the library by Black friends who weren't friends—usually the boys in grade eleven when I was in grade twelve, the boys I played sports with after school and sometimes hung out with at the Burger King at lunch, the boys who were my boys but weren't really my boys—they asked questions. Rhetorical questions that aimed to sting me but revealed their truth. Their insecurities. Mine too. Black friends would skip earnest lines by asking rehearsed ones, like, "Yo, who the hell are you trying to be?"

Mahmoud asked me that same question in the library one time. I laughed him off by answering, "Yo, who the fuck you think you are, yo?" It was serious for a moment. We stared at each other, blaming each other for betraying our Blackness, the very thing school taught us to do. We were checking on each other's Blackness because it was what we had learned to do. Through school. Because of school. After a tense few seconds, we both chuckled. In my head, I could hear a laugh track signalling all was well. I'm sure he could too. He walked into the stacks. He wasn't about to leave the library. Neither was I.

MY TYPA NIGGA

I never hid anything from Mom. I was fourteen when I told her I wanted to pierce my ear. She asked why. I listed a bunch of men I looked up to who had an earring: Michael Jordan, Tupac, Jay-Z, and Ken Griffey Jr. She said okay. We walked to the hair salon at the corner of Scarborough Golf Club Road and Lawrence Avenue the following weekend. She gave $10 to the Chinese hairdresser who asked me three times which ear I wanted pierced. Left, left ear, the left one. The piercing gun snapped and I felt a sharp pinch. She told us that I needed to keep the piercing clean with rubbing alcohol and not to take out the stud for at least two weeks. I couldn't wait to go home and look at myself in the mirror.

When I twirled the nickel-free stainless steel stud in my left earlobe, I felt bigger. Taller. My boys looked at me differently. Maybe with more conviction. Like I was Blacker. The snap of that gun instantly drew me closer to who I wanted to be. Soon as my piercing healed, I begged Mom to take me to Cedarbrae Mall. She asked why. I told her that Puff Daddy, Will Smith, Snoop Dogg, and Emmitt Smith didn't wear stainless steel in their ears: they wore *diamonds*. "But I'll take one that costs twenty bucks instead," I told her. That weekend we walked up to the jewellery stand in the mall and I picked out a fat square-cut earring that glistened. The silver-plated cubic zirconia cost her $10.

At home I stared into the mirror for at least thirty minutes after I put it in. I slightly tilted my head to the right when I posed for my student card photo that fall. I needed everyone to see that small new part of me. I wanted to show off. Mom didn't mind. She knew she had to gradually relinquish my body. Dad minded. He asked me when I was going to start wearing dresses; he called me a faggot every now and then when he had too many drinks. I shrugged off his insults. I knew he didn't know what a young nigga born in the mid-'80s was supposed to look like. He thought Bill Cosby was still the shit.

Looking back, I see that I was attempting to construct my own Blackness from the images blitzed before me. My idea of what a Black man ought to be came through the culture that surrounded me, and I bombarded my body with markers of Black masculinity that told me how to be a man and how to be Black. How to be a Black man. My childhood edification came from messages I received from all those men I'd named to my mom. Those men spoke to me even though they didn't directly address me.

Those men kept showing and teaching and telling. I kept listening. When the peach fuzz above my top lip darkened into a thin mustache, I knew I was old enough to get my other ear pierced. Right, right ear, the right one. Graduating from a sterling stud to another fake diamond felt more natural this time, and faster. I scratched off the scab and pushed that fake diamond through because I needed the next marker of Black manhood on my body sooner rather than later. I knew it would heal regardless. For my next student card photo, I didn't have to tilt my head either way. They would see me. See what I wanted to be. It was inevitable.

"Ma, me and Tucker are going to the tattoo parlour in a couple hours. I'm gonna get something on my shoulder," I said near the end of grade ten. I had been drumming up the courage to raise the topic for a few weeks. I decided that I would tell her instead of asking.

"No, you're not," she responded, without even lifting her gaze from the dishes she was washing in the sink. I shrugged her off. Tucker's older brother had already agreed to sign the consent papers for us; we were only sixteen, not old enough to legally make decisions about our own bodies. Technically still boys, but grown enough to think we no longer needed permission to modify our outsides. "No way in hell you're living under my roof with tattoos on your skin," she said. When Mom really meant something, she ended her sentences with my name. I sensed an opportunity.

I sensed that my opaque intention impeded the conversation I really needed to have with her. Although I felt like I was grown and didn't need permission from her—from anyone—I still needed acknowledgment. Especially from her.

"The appointment is at seven p.m., Mom. *In God's Hands.* That's what I'm getting, Mom. Just on the top of my shoulder. You know, those words have a good meaning. So much meaning. I won't ever regret it," I argued. "What do you think?"

She still didn't look at me. "Matthew, no. Your dad will kill you if he sees a fucking tattoo on your arm." She finally put down the fork she was rinsing and looked at me. "He doesn't even like you having earrings. He thinks they mean you're gay." I stared back, but a smirk snuck through. She couldn't help but chuckle before turning back to the dishes. It wasn't permission, but it was acknowledgment. Exactly what I needed.

The tattoo gun sent shivers through my whole body when it first pierced my skin. A thousand times sharper than what I'd felt in my earlobe. It was like biting into a deep-fried Snickers bar at the CNE and feeling all the oily batter, salt, and sugar rush toward the pores of your face. I contemplated telling the artist to stop. To forget it and I'd pay anyway. I didn't think I would be able to endure the pain; maybe Mom knew something I didn't. But Tucker had already sat through his session, a full hour, while his brother laughed at the sweat beading under his toque. He now had the words *He Got Game* scribed into his skin, dedicated to his love for basketball and his favourite movie. He'd manned up so I couldn't be a pussy.

Fifty minutes later, the tattoo artist put down the ink gun and wiped the blood and excess ink off my skin with paper towels. He rubbed my new inscription with Vaseline, covered it with a medical bandage, and slung Saran wrap over my shoulder and under my armpit. He gave us instructions on how to keep our new ink clean so it healed properly: no strenuous activity for a day, no direct sun, no scented lotions, no pools.

Instead of heading home, Tucker and I went to the local church to hoop at the Friday night ball runs. We didn't know that when sweat mixed with petroleum jelly, it loosened adhesives. The tattoo artist had told us to keep the bandage on for a few hours and remove it when we showered. But after three or four games of basketball, the constant fidgeting and resetting of the protective wrap on our skin grew pointless. Tucker took his off first. I followed shortly after.

We couldn't wait to show off our tattoos anyway. We rolled our T-shirt sleeves up like tank tops. When I angled my arm, my permanent ink glistened. Our boys studied our tattoos with appreciation. It felt like we had broken some new ground on becoming men. On becoming Black men. I told them to step back when they played defence too close.

Mom was watching television when I got home. I locked the front door and walked past her to the kitchen to warm up my dinner. I avoided her eyes, wanting to hide this new part of me for as long as I could. A tattoo wouldn't kill her, but I didn't want to hurt her.

Not everyone I looked up to pierced their ears or inked their skin. But those modifications were the most easily identifiable markers of Black masculinity that I aspired to as a teen. Once I made those first two alterations, I began to look for more. Subtler ways of silently articulating what the skin I was in meant to me.

My brother needed corrective shoes to learn how to walk when he was a toddler. I didn't. My parents told me that I picked up physical coordination rather easily. Moving my body smoothly and powerfully came to me naturally from an early age. I remember studying the stances of baseball players in the batter's box when I was young enough to still fantasize of playing for the Toronto Blue Jays one day. These men swung for the fences, and when they got a direct boom on that baseball, their home run trots were fantastical to me. Something not to be duplicated unless you were strutting around bases on a diamond. LeShawn's older brother didn't play sports, but he had a way of walking that soothed my eyes. There was nothing intentional in the way he moved. Nothing pronounced, nothing sporty. It felt airy and underplayed. So understated that there was nothing about it that warranted studying. Just a stroke that I saw. Maybe that's why I wanted to emulate it. I wanted to look like I wasn't even trying.

I noticed other older boys who glided with the same precision. It had been years since Mom led me by hand to and from grocery stores, malls, and parent-teacher interviews. Now that I was on the brink of fully claiming my body from her, it was as if I had to learn how to walk again. And this time, I had to do it without falling or looking stupid.

Practice was clearly unnecessary. LeShawn's brother never practised how to walk once he became a man. Neither did my favourite rappers or athletes. Practising would be corny. They just walked. I would learn through osmosis.

Adjusting my outside—piercing ears, tattooing skin, walking with a nuanced gait, talking with a local accent, and using slang—was cosmetic and relatively easy. Rearranging my inside took more work.

Both were required of me if I wanted to be Black like all the other Black men I looked up to. At family barbecues on apartment balconies, back porches, or front verandas, uncles and older male cousins would ask my pops, "Yo, when is Matthew going to start smoking weed?" I was confused and a bit embarrassed. I didn't understand what their question meant. Was I not a man if I didn't smoke weed? Was smoking weed a rite of passage to prove my masculinity? Would I be less than if I chose not to smoke weed? Would I be less Black?

Questions like that made anxiety churn inside me, and it was only soothed by some sense of how to reconcile with Blackness—my Blackness. A trip down to Detroit for a family reunion in the summer heading into grade nine gave me some answers.

I shoved my backpack full of clothes into the trunk of our used 1994 Ford Tempo and placed my Panasonic Shockwave CD player on the passenger-side back seat. That was our way of claiming space. Tiny and I had a habit of fighting over meaningless things like spots on the couch. Me wanting a particular seat in the car seemed to be the only motivation my little brother needed to try to take it. It was like he had to be where I was. Looking back, I think he was gathering all the little clues about how to be, just like I was soaking up lessons from the older men around me. Inside the house, Dad was huddled over the kitchen counter pouring a beer into a Thermos while Mom stalked every room, double-checking that lights were off and cords were unplugged from outlets.

"Okay, almost ready," Mom declared. "Just want to check the lights in the basement one more time."

Dad, Tiny, and I made our way to the car.

"Can we switch seats when we stop for gas on the highway?" Tiny asked. "You always get to sit there."

"Nah, yo. What's the difference?" I responded. Now I knew I had to remain in that spot when we stopped or get back to the car before he did if we both got out.

"Fucking asshole," Tiny blurted.

"Aye! Una watch your bloodclat language," Dad said as he worked on nestling his Thermos between his legs and out of sight. "Matthew, go see what yuh mom doing. We need to get on the road so we can get there before night."

"Alright. Tiny, I'll let you sit here when we stop for gas." I stepped out, knowing that I would break my promise. Inside, Mom was pressing the stove dials in the off position and staring at them intently, as if eye contact and prolonged human touch would ensure our house wouldn't burn down while we were gone. "They're off, Mom," I told her gently. "Dad says we gotta go if we're going to get to Detroit before dark."

"Okay, okay. Just let me go pee one more time, and we'll leave. Go wait in the car. Two minutes." Before heading to the bathroom, she repeated her ritual on the refrigerator. She pressed her palms back and forth between the handles of the fridge and freezer doors to make sure they were sealed. "Two minutes," she said.

Twenty minutes later, she wiggled the knob on the front door to make sure she had locked it and then got into the passenger seat. Our four-hour trip to Detroit—to America, to meet some of my African American relatives—was finally underway.

It seemed like a hundred American flags swayed against the blue sky as we approached the border. I thought about how I would greet my American cousins. In the back seat of the car, I silently mimicked the New York accents of Jay-Z and Nas. I imagined my cousins not noticing the differences between their Black culture and my mosaic one. I wondered if they would ask if we turned off the stove and checked the fridge twice before leaving our igloo.

Rolling my window down to get a closer look at downtown Detroit left me slightly stunned. It looked like a scene from *New Jack City*. So many boarded-up windows and broken-down buildings. So, this is America, I thought. Black America. Real Black. Real broken.

I tried to imagine what it would be like to have grown up in Detroit instead of Scarborough. Life would have undoubtedly been different, I thought. I would have been a real nigga if I *had* to live here.

Aunt Mavis's house was actually in Oak Park, Michigan. A nice house, nicer than ours back in Canada. It wasn't exactly Detroit. Thirteen miles away. I didn't know that then. All I knew was that I couldn't wait to sit with and talk to and learn from my cousins, especially the one I had heard so much about—Khaliff.

"You're going to love Khaliff. You're just like him," my cousin Shelly had told me ever since I was a child. "He has a bit more charm, but you two have the same personality, I swear." She'd say stuff like that at family barbecues before my uncles would ask Dad questions about me and weed and coming of age.

"Wassup, lil cuz," Khaliff said as he dapped me. He hugged Mom and watched her gravitate over to Mavis, his mom. "Look at this little light-skin nigga . . . You must pull all the little badass bitches at your school, huh?" Then he dapped my brother and gave my dad a hug.

"He hasn't told me about any," dad said. "I think he's one of them batty bwoys. Man went and got an earring."

Both Khaliff and Dad chuckled, not really needing me to respond. I just half-smiled at Khaliff and rolled my eyes at Dad while faking a left jab to his ribs. He didn't flinch. His reactions were a bit delayed; he'd refilled his Thermos two or three times during our trip.

"I'm gonna meet one of my boys. Say, y'all wanna roll?" The way Khaliff dropped the hard consonants off words fascinated me. Rolling sounded so cool, so authentically Black. Better than "Do you guys want to come with me?" Less pedantic and more American, more real. I made a mental note to use *roll* or *rolling* instead of *go* or *going*. I couldn't wait to spend more time in Detroit—Oak Park—and I couldn't wait to get back home to Canada to talk at my boys in new ways.

"C'mon. We out," he said as my dad, Tiny, and I walked with him to his 1996 cherry-red Honda Civic hatchback. I glanced back at our Ford Tempo. So measly in comparison. Made for Bill Cosby type of niggas. Khaliff, on the other hand, with his Civic, his suave Black demeanour, his clear Black skin, and the fresh sentences that came out of his Black American mouth made gliding to that back seat effortless. I let Tiny pick what side he wanted to sit on. I was feeling magnanimous.

His boy was at a hotel. We pulled into the Ramada off Franklin Road and took the elevator up to a room where hip-hop blasted through thin walls. His boy opened the door and the heavy breeze of weed smoke brushed my face. Maybe I did need to smoke weed to become a Black man. His boy had company—a naked girl on the bed who didn't make any rushed attempt to cover herself. Maybe I was gay like Dad jabbed. So cool was Khaliff that he didn't even introduce us to his friends, something I thought was standard. He just sat on the edge of the other bed and talked about a sale he'd made earlier that day. I had so much to learn.

For the next hour I sat in a desk chair in the corner while Khaliff, his boy, and my dad talked. Tiny took a spot on the opposite side of the bed that Khaliff was sitting on. He faced me while occasionally glancing over his shoulder at Khaliff's friend and the woman who now had covered her upper body with a baggy white T-shirt. Me and Tiny made awkward small talk with each other—about what we packed in our backpacks and what our friends might be up to back home. That kept us comfortable in this new foreign environment. We weren't really listening to each other but our words provided a blanket for us to hide under and watch without being noticed. A cover to cloak us while we observed with our Canadian eyes what the land of the free and the home of the brave really meant for Black men like my cousin.

We got back to Aunt Mavis's house just as the summer sun was setting. "Y'all don't talk much, huh?" Khaliff said while pulling into his driveway. "That shy shit is aiight, but it'll only take you so far in life. Especially out here." He had read everything he needed to know about us in that hotel room, and he was positioning himself to teach us a few things during our stay. Like how to be Black. I knew I had lots to see, hear, and soak up. Shelly was right. I was going to love Khaliff. I was already admiring all the pieces that made up who he was. But Shelly was also wrong: I wasn't just like him. His Blackness oozed out of him so effortlessly. Mine fell in forced rivulets. I watched him intently, and I cherished my time in his presence. It meant so many things to me. Among them, the opportunity to percolate.

I first felt Black because of something I lacked. Black by omission. Before I asked Mom for permission to get an earring or begged her to buy me Snoop Dogg's *Doggystyle* album, I wanted a hairstyle like a teen pop celebrity—Jonathan Taylor Thomas or Leonardo DiCaprio. Boy bands like New Kids on the Block and the actors on shows like *90210* cornered popular masculine imagery at the same time I started becoming attracted to the girls in my third grade class. All of my boys had those hairstyles and I wanted to do the same—to fit in with my boys.

So I declined trips with Dad to the barber in the hopes that my hair would grow long enough to part it in the middle and let it fall to the side over my ears. At seven or eight years old, I didn't consider that '90s-style heartthrob cut a white or Black thing. It was around me by virtue of the all-white classrooms I attended. The white side of pop culture birthed it, and because I was around that side, I wanted to duplicate it.

Despite the mousse and gel Mom bought for me, my hair never sat down. The longer it grew, the higher it sprouted. Instead of looking like those bleached-blond child stars, I looked more like Kid from the hip-hop duo Kid 'n Play. The trip to Conrad's barbershop became essential. I asked for a one level high fade with a part in the front. I'd learned that certain things about my body were different from the white boys I was boys with. I'd finally accepted what my body—and television, music, and media—had long been whispering. Black is Black is Black. And Black is different, whether I wanted to accept the heavy drops I had or not.

Welcoming it provided relief. I was no longer trying to be what I wasn't. And now there were new markers to emulate. Even those fixed definitions of Blackness provided me with wiggle room to choose. Learning that I was Black was the easy part. Wrestling with what Blackness, Black boyhood, and Black manhood meant took work from the inside out. It wasn't as easy as getting a mushroom cut or frosting my tips and carrying on with my day like the white boys I was friends with. In the early '90s, becoming Black meant becoming a nigga. And becoming a nigga made for complicated decisions and precarious conditions.

Khaliff took me and Tiny to the mall the next afternoon, in Detroit. At twenty-four, he straddled the older generation of Dad and my aunt Mavis and the energetic group of teenagers who gathered at our family reunion. At thirteen, I couldn't shake a subtle fear as we walked through that mall. America, Black America, had become synonymous with danger and crime and erratic behaviour in my mind. Every Black man looked like a threat to me. It didn't seem like Khaliff, or even Tiny, carried the same trepidation as we strolled from store to store. The fact that I couldn't flush this feeling was disappointing. I constantly reminded myself that the Black men in these stores with their pants low and hats tilted were shoppers, not killers or drug dealers or gangbangers. I couldn't wait to get back to Aunt Mavis's home in Oak Park, to stare in the mirror at my own reflection. To reassure myself that I, too, was Black.

I studied the new baseball hat Khaliff bought me when I got back into the front seat of his red Civic. Tiny got in the back. He'd gotten Dr. Dre's new CD, *The Chronic 2001*. Being in that two-door hatchback made me feel safe again. Khaliff checked his pager and said, "I gotta stop at a few spots before we head back. Y'all niggas cool with that?" Despite being in his early twenties, he talked to us like we were on his level. I felt even safer. Because now I was inches closer to the reassurance I needed about who I was.

"No problem . . . nigga." I had been saying *that* word to my new friends in middle school over the last two years, and it had become casual to me now. Saying it this time, to Khaliff, felt deliberate.

Khaliff weaved through Detroit, stopping at multiple houses, hotels, and homes to connect with people he knew. Most of them were women. He studied an envelope scribbled with names and numbers and, remembering that we were in the car too, asked, "So, yo, how many girlfriends you got, Matt?"

I knew I had to pass his test. "A few. The main one is Alisha," I answered. Alisha had been one of my very first girlfriends, but we only dated for two months at the beginning of grade eight. We'd broken up a few months prior. I hoped I'd passed the litmus test.

"Okay, cool. Shorty you just met is one of mine. We going to see Bianca right now, another one."

"You're a player, eh." I immediately regretted my words. An admission that I didn't know things about being a nigga that I ought to know at my age.

"Eh?" He laughed. "Y'all Canadians really do say that shit, huh." I sat silently. There was no way to redeem what I just lost. "I keep a few around. I'm still young, man. You're a young nigga; you gotta keep your options open too."

"Alright" was the only word I could muster.

After leaving Bianca's basement, Khaliff unwrapped the new CD he bought for himself and slid it into the disc changer. "Y'all know Ruff Ryders, right?"

"Course, nigga. They're all over the radio back home." This time the word slipped through my lips a bit more naturally. They actually weren't all over the radio back in Canada, but I knew who they were—a collection of hip-hop artists creating a new hip-hop wave and fan base, one that I paid close attention to.

The first song off the compilation album blared through his subwoofers. The bass was so loud I could barely hear myself think. By the time we got off the highway and onto the main roads of Oak Park, the fourth track had started. Jay-Z's "Jigga My Nigga" began with bellowing tugboat horns. With the car windows down, it felt as if Khaliff's little red Civic hatchback was the only car on the road that mattered. Every other car was just in the way. I snuck a look at my older cousin. I watched the way his left hand gripped the steering wheel, the way his torso casually reclined at a forty-five-degree angle in his tilted-back car seat, and the way he glanced peripherally through his sunglasses at the cars beside him and the people on the sidewalks. Rolling down those streets, he became the centre of attention—almost as if he commanded it. As if *he* was in a music video. And by virtue of his presence, his

Blackness, and my proximity, I was caught up in that recognition. I relished the feeling.

Khaliff hit repeat on that song again and again. For the last fifteen minutes of the drive back home, that four-minute-and-forty-second song played on a loop. Each time I gained more confidence in my body, my hair, my skin. I nodded my head as the hook reverberated through the muggy air. I was with my family. Safe. Driving. Rollin' with my niggas. I didn't need to get in front of a mirror to remind myself of who I was.

I'd felt the dissonance between *who* I was and *what* I was long before I rolled through Detroit with Khaliff and long after I returned home to Canada with my family. The close bonds I had with the white Ronnie Reeds and David Stones of primary school evaporated around the same time those boy bands like NSYNC and Backstreet Boys were breaking up. But whereas Justin Timberlake—like David or Ronnie—was able to carve out a solo career and exist on his own as an individual with a white scalp and frosted tips, I belonged to a collective and I faded my hair and accented my body with earrings and tattoos. Although I *wanted* to belong to that collective, I quickly learned that I couldn't escape from it.

While the white boys I used to play baseball and have sleepovers with could experiment with their images while still remaining individual, my choices were filtered through the inescapable reality of belonging to a category. A visible minority. White boys could wear their hair long or shave it off; either way they were still recognized, called by their first names. Before I got my first tattoo, I was marked by being Black.

Learning I was Black meant learning that whatever action I took would be scrutinized. I saw that scrutiny in the eyes of others. Once I started to devote serious energy to my schoolwork in grade twelve, teachers would approach me after handing back an assignment:

"Matthew, this was really good. Good for you. If you keep this up, you'll do really well in this class." As if completing their assignments was a challenging feat for a Black boy like me. As if doing well made me extraordinary compared to other Black boys. Did these same grown white people wonder at the bodies of people like Martin Luther King Jr.? Did they wonder if only I'd erase my tattoos and let the holes in my ears close, I could be a one-off like him?

Sometimes I wondered the same thing. Was I pushing the so-called limits of Black excellence? The same limits that gave them, my white teachers, the privilege of considering me to be the exception to the rule at times and the rule itself at others? Black men like Martin Luther King Jr. were clearly the exception. His ingenuity was a once-in-a-lifetime thing—an anomaly. He was remarkable for any man, let alone a Black one. Even I, a teenager, could see that. Couldn't these white teachers understand the same thing when they showed me how *surprised* they were by my intelligence? Intelligent enough to lift me out of the Black box they had put me in and congratulate me on my willingness to achieve. Didn't they see that I looked up to Black men like Martin Luther King Jr. *and* Black men like Martin Lawrence? Didn't they see that I looked up to realistic, less idealized versions of Black men simply because I saw more of those types of niggas on TV? Because I listened to more of those type of niggas through eight-by-ten speakers in red Civics and watched them chillin' in parks and malls in Scarborough?

I didn't love Martin as much as I loved Will, but we loved *Martin* as much as we loved *The Fresh Prince*. In the '90s, both characters captured our imaginations. Between those two men, for us, it was simply a matter of preference. Jay-Z also captivated us. Captivated me. But as I got older, I ran through my fantastical world of Black potential and possibility, searching for symbols that could gain me acceptance. Tattoos, earrings, hats worn to the back, sitting at a forty-five-degree angle while driving Dad's powder-blue used Buick Regal—all these things made me simultaneously fit in and stand out. Fit in as a Black man and stand out to others who weren't Black.

Performing popular notions of Black manliness was uppermost in our minds, living as we did in Canada, where the majority of the population was devoted to hockey stats, winter tires, and ending their sentences with the word *eh*. Existing as a Black Canadian boy, then young man, in the late '90s to the early 2000s meant belonging to an ascribed family, but one that didn't entirely claim us. Our lack of kinship to the clan that resided north of the forty-ninth parallel didn't necessarily unnerve us; it was the ambivalence from our Black American brethren that was disconcerting. We did not share unpretentious lineage with our white Canadian friends, their fathers, and neighbours. But for those of us who grew up on hip-hop, sports, and most things Black, we felt as if our real roots somehow traced back along those invisible railroads buried deep underground and headed straight south. Khaliff was my cousin, related by blood. We were family. But geography stripped us of familiarity. Our Black Canadian selves wanted a hug from our more polished African American big bros. But those born on the other side of the border neglected us. Not on purpose, but for the sake of their singularity. We couldn't understand it then. So, for years we saw ourselves in the family portrait but on the periphery of the group, like adopted sons, fostered by parents across the border. Close in proximity and shade but apart by nationality and true culture. I felt then that I needed to earn my spot in the portrait. Being a first-generation Black Canadian left me feeling I had to prove that I had the right to be one of the niggas.

About a year after my first tattoo, I decided it was time to grow my collection. Finally past the legal age of consent in Ontario, we no longer needed to ask for permission or get an older brother to sign forms for us. Before I left for the same tattoo parlour on Kingston Road, I told Mom my intentions again. Again she advised against it, reminding me of the same things she'd warned me about a year prior: Tattoos were permanent; I could get a disease or infection from a dirty needle; Dad would be pissed. But this time she mentioned stereotypes, and how boys who look like me might be put in a category by others as men with a bad reputation. "I'm just saying, Matthew. These things matter. They'll start to look at you a certain way just because you have tattoos." She was acknowledging that the David Stones and Ronnie Reeds of the world could manipulate their bodies and still be recognized as Ronnie and David first, but that once *I* did, I'd be trapped in the category that they wanted to put me in anyways.

"I know, Mom. I know," I said as I walked out of the kitchen toward the front door. We both knew she was right, but neither hair gel nor winter weather in Canada would ever work for me.

"You really shouldn't get another tattoo, Matthew. It's bad for your skin, anyways. They say that, you know."

I knew, I knew. And I really wanted to ask Mom, "What's the difference?" My skin would forever be a hazard to my health. But I could never be that bold. I could never be that cynical or lost. I knew, but I didn't need to tell her what I thought she knew too.

"It'll be alright, Mom. It's safe. I'm safe," I said as I put on my shoes.

"Be safe, Matthew," she said.

I decided that this time I would get my nickname, Parkay, scrolled down my left bicep. Tucker was doing the same. At first I'd hated my nickname. Like most Black boys, my nickname came from my peers' careful observation of my obvious inadequacies. Some of my friends had nicknames like Weezy or Cube because they resembled Black celebrities; others earned their nicknames through oxymoronic juxtapositions, like my brother who at age eleven was 215 pounds and received his nickname Tiny. Some garnered their second labels through the physical characteristics that came to define them. I know three men with the nickname Short Man or Shorts—all of them five foot five or under—and four men with the nickname Scars or Scar. All of these men eventually grew to wear their nicknames like a second skin. Some of us decided to get them permanently marked on our bodies.

I knew I wanted Parkay on my left bicep; the only thing I needed to figure out was the font. I scrolled through the tattoo book looking for the perfect style that would be different enough to stand out but recognizable enough for my people, my niggas, to recognize. I settled on a bamboo font that looked Chinese, like some of the tattoos on Allen Iverson's body. This time, I went first. While the tattoo artist drilled his ink gun into my arm, Tucker joked with me to keep my mind off the pain.

"Yo, P. We ahead of the game. Second tattoo already, and we aren't even finished high school yet? These niggas got a lot of catching up to do." He laughed.

"I think they're scared of the pain, bro," I lamented. "We should roll to the basketball courts after this. Show these off. Nothing crazy flashy, you know? But let them know, eh." I wanted to roll after this pain was over. I knew he wanted to get rollin' right after he finished too. We both wanted to endure. And then roll. To earn our proof. So they could see that we were indeed etching ourselves toward those typa niggas.

When it was his turn, I watched Tucker occasionally hide grimaces as the needle dotted his skin. To keep his mind off the pain, we argued about who was funnier—Chris Tucker or Chris Rock. I knew I would never win an argument with him regarding anything pertaining to Chris Tucker; he was the reason we never called Richard by his given name.

Mom rolled her eyes and shook her head weeks later when she eventually noticed my nickname on my arm. She always called me by the name she gave me and only referred to me as Parkay when she wanted to get some point across. One time I reminded her why I was still in bed at seven thirty one morning, instead of getting ready for school, and she said, "Oh, you got suspended for two days because you didn't take your hat off after they asked you to, twice. Nice one, *Parkay*." Another time: "How come I never see you reading anymore? You used to beg me every time a Scholastic flyer came home to buy you an R. L. Stine. What happened? Does *Parkay* not know how to read?"

After seeing that nickname etched permanently on my arm, Mom never used it to ask me a rhetorical question. She never poked me about it. She seemed to know what it meant to me. I never wanted to hurt her either, so I never attempted to make it make sense to her. I trusted that I would be able to *show* her that I was safe. I hoped that what I continued to do, inside and out, would keep me safe.

It did, slowly. Thanks to the other niggas I saw around me—or didn't see. I didn't see LeShawn's older brother anymore, because he, like a lot of niggas I looked up to, ended up out of sight. Either locked up in cages or locked down inside pine boxes.

I visited Khaliff a few more times in Detroit. By then, at seventeen, eighteen, I could show him how I'd become a nigga too. I could finally talk about girls and girlfriends without lying. I could tell him that I didn't smoke weed, not because I was afraid of it, but because it made me paranoid. A sentiment I didn't have to explain further, regardless of whether we were talking about drugs or not. A trip and revelation that he could laugh at but also respect. A shared bridge that we could mutually meet at. It was what I was looking for. Belonging.

Khaliff even came up to Toronto one weekend in the summer when I was eighteen. I drove him around in Dad's powder-blue Buick Regal, laughing about how fast I used to think he drove when I was thirteen. I gripped the steering wheel with my left hand. I tilted my seat back. I blasted Jay-Z's newest CD, *The Blueprint 2*. Over and over, we listened to the track "U Don't Know." Pulling back up to my parents' home, I kept thinking, They really don't know, eh. They really don't know.

Khaliff's trip to Toronto that summer was the last time I saw him. A few years before that, Shelly had told me that Khaliff had sickle cell anemia. "It's a disease that only Black people can get, cousin. We're genetically predisposed to it. Part of our culture," she taught me. When I asked her more, she said, "Not like cancer. But it is a blood disorder, from what I know. He's got to go to the hospital every now and then when things get low. It's a Black thing, cousin. Just one of those things our people could be born with." She also mentioned limited life expectancy. I never asked why. I knew why. I knew.

Months after I got to drive Khaliff around in Scarborough, Shelly was on the other end of the house phone when I picked up. "Cousin. I love you. Cousin, I have to tell you something. Your cousin Khaliff is dead, cousin."

"What?" The phone was mounted on the wall that jutted out between our kitchen and living room. I stood there at a loss for words. I thought about his disease and how sick it was that this ailment, so specific and unfair to Black people, had killed him. "What?" I asked again.

"Yes. He has passed away," she said. She seemed shocked to hear herself speak those words. "In a better place now." She paused. "Let me talk to your mom, cousin."

Time stopped. My insides froze. After time started again, I called for Mom. After I handed her the phone, I lingered in the kitchen, listening. Running to Tiny to repeat things I heard, telling him I wasn't lying, looking at Dad enjoying his food with his eyes closed while sports commentators described play by play the game on the TV. I was listening to Mom, but I was seeing a shiny red Civic hatchback, hearing Jigga's bravado and bass, seeing coolness embodied in a man who no longer existed. Shaking my head. Saying no. No. No.

We drove back to Detroit the following week. I listened with Tiny, underneath that invisible blanket we'd first shared in the Ramada years earlier, to hushed conversations on the driveway at Aunt Mavis's house in Oak Park. Conversations about making sales while recalling the smell of weed inside a cheap hotel. Conversations about a knife. A girl. "Yeah, they owed him money. I told him not to ever go back around there. That's why we moved to Oak Park. That place in Detroit is so hood. Fulla niggers." Jealousy. "They did try to steal the Civic before, yes. Clean through the heart. One stab wound. Direct." Murder. "He was doing so well despite that sickle cell. Sold cars at the GM dealership. Damn good job of it too. Employee of the month. Making good money, honest money. Graduated Wayne State." Heads nodded slowly. "Dead on arrival." Tears fell slowly. My head rang.

Khaliff's wake was the first time I saw a dead body in real life. I waited for him to get up out of the glossy oak box he was in. I waited for so long, frozen on my feet. Until I had to grab Tiny and rub his back to get him to stop shaking and screaming. Mom was right: he was just a kid. We both were.

Knowing that someone I knew, someone who was family, someone I looked up to, who taught me how to be, had been *murdered* did something to me. Something so small that I did not notice until long after my insides thawed the second time.

I was taking courses in college classrooms where no one cared what type of nigga I was. It was around 2008. Me and Tucker and my boys from high school still did things we always did. Eventually I got more ink, trying to hide the psychic scars from years and years of listening to and looking at my type of niggas. But my professors didn't tell me how shocked they were at my mix of urban Black semblance with Black common sense, because they had Barack to look to. They saw him shake hands with white guys and dap Black niggas. They'd watched Tupac and Biggie succumb to the same fate as Khaliff to be replaced by Kanye and Drake and other singing and rapping niggas who didn't share sonic stories about guns and gangs and ravaging through girls. They took notice of Michael Jordan's retirement and witnessed LeBron James rise straight from high school to the pinnacle of sport and never once screw up profession-ally or personally. The type of niggas I watched from a distance in the '90s had been overtaken by a type of Black masculinity that was a bit softer around the edges. I was lucky. Lucky to be born at a time when I could start to grow into my name, my nickname, and my Blackness, and still be somewhat safe.

Somewhat.

Some of those white teachers, those white professors, showed us that we were safe. We got comfortable through the degrees we earned and the ways we corrected our speech to show them that we, too, deserve a seat at the table and a small slice of the pie. We showed them that we could do right by their standards. And just when we thought we were out of danger, some of them pulled us back in. Reminded us that we were scarred. Reminded us that we were not really beloved by them.

Years after Khaliff's red Civic boomed bass through my ear-drums, I rolled to work where I tried to teach kids basic grade seven shit. Mom was proud. I'd graduated university and got a job as a teacher. The career I'd built proved what I had long told her. That I would be safe. That I wouldn't degenerate. That despite the ink and the layers of clothing and the layered walk, I could be

Matthew and Parkay and be accepted for my first name first. I didn't quite believe it myself, but I had long fought to prove to her that it was possible. I didn't see earrings or tattoos or even Black skin on any of my colleagues, but that meant that I could show, rather than tell, her that there was a healthy gap between the type of niggas she saw on television screens and what she saw in my Black body.

I thought I was out; I thought I was safe—until Ken reminded me I wasn't. He was like most of the other white men I met when I started teaching: he wanted to give me room but also wanted to chew away at the clean Black space I cultivated. When we began talking at work, in school, I felt that he felt we existed on the same level. He didn't remind me of Mr. Turner and the older white men who had treated me like a Black man when I was only a kid. Ken allowed me to *think* that I'd earned equal footing with his white self. Every now and then he surprised me by doing right—asking about my life without apparent judgment, asking me about our work like I had something to teach *him*. He started asking about my family, about all these personal things without asking for those small pieces of counsel and advice that made me feel safe. Respected. Eventually, he asked about my tattoos and the reasons behind them.

I didn't take it personally when he asked questions about marks on my skin or the clothes I wore to cover some of them up. That was the reason I initially got them: to draw attention to me and my Blackness. To make apparent the group of men I belonged to. To appear on the outside in ways I grew to learn would settle me inside. I wanted easy ways to demonstrate the main pieces of my identity, so I picked clothes, and gold, and earrings, and tattoos. Along with that came choosing coded communication, muzzling my speech, and modifying my steps. I did so in the hopes that such questions would be more rhetorical than direct and personal. After Detroit and then college, after I'd firmly established myself in my career as a teacher, I assumed my presence as the type of nigga I looked up to would come with objective acknowledgment. I never thought that white men like Ken would still attempt to rub my Blackness in my face.

After Ken and I became friendly enough for me to be comfortable around him, I saw how my assumptions, my craving to belong in both worlds, and my learning were not as black and white as I'd presumed.

Encountering Ken in the school hallway one spring afternoon revealed the dire positions that Black boys like me found ourselves in—regardless of how many tattoos we got or how many degrees we earned or how much we'd grown up.

I'd just finished a chicken wrap and a Gatorade and left the staffroom to head back to my classroom on the second floor. Instead of taking the closest stairs, I decided to walk to the far end. The only men's bathroom was at the east end of the school and I had made after-lunch urination something of a routine. It was the only way I could teach from twelve to three without a break. I usually ran into Ken while walking down that first-floor hallway. He always seemed to be outside his classroom then, doing goofy things that he thought lightened the mood—playing his guitar or dancing to music in a cringe-inducing way.

This time as I approached from a good forty feet away, I noticed there was no music playing and he was guitar-less. I put my head down awkwardly, because making and maintaining eye contact for all that distance seemed way too unnatural. His "Yooo, yo!" forced my head up. I watched as Ken, walking toward me, pulled his baseball cap to the side. "Yooo, yo! Yo, Matt, what's up, dog?" My eyes grew wide as he tugged down his weathered cargo shorts and changed his stride to have a severe lean to the right and a heavy limp every time his left foot struck the floor.

"Yo, yo," he repeated while holding his arms out and sprawling his fingers.

My brain went blank; I didn't know what to do. Was he trying to acknowledge me in some innocent comical way? Was he trying to imitate what I projected on a daily basis at work, as a teacher, as a Black man? I didn't walk like that, did I? No, no, I didn't; it couldn't be that. I know I definitely didn't talk like that, especially not at work. Especially not around white people. I had learned long ago how to muzzle myself in professional settings. Did he want me to laugh at his caricature? Approve of his mockery? Or did he want me to tell him to fuck off so that he could really get off his chest what he thought about me? About Black boys who grew up to be men like me? Too many questions flooded my mind with too little distance between us to process them. I raised my eyebrows and flashed a half smile as we passed each other, his white face playing at blackface for reasons I could not understand.

I let the moment sit with me for days before telling anyone. After mentioning it to my boys, they said things like, "Only a matter of time, bro" and "That's white people for ya. They think we're all the same." We nodded in recognition to new and old stories about them stereotyping us and shackling our identities to our skin colour.

They think we're all the same.

They all think that we're all the same.

We sat there expounding on our thoughts about them. Specifically about how they thought about us. About how we thought that they thought that we were all just the same. The sting of Ken's performance lessened as my boys and I talked about *them* through *him*. Ken confirmed our feelings; his performance rationalized the shields we put on, made sense of all the safety mechanisms we'd developed. It felt right to believe that they had the same feelings about all of us. We didn't realize that we were thinking the same about all the white Kens that we'd encountered all of our lives.

I don't know if all the tattoos and piercings and jewellery and ways of walking and talking turned me into the type of nigga I always wanted to be. Or if it would have happened without those things.

Mom was right all along. The last time we met in the kitchen after I got another tattoo gave me clarity. Clarity about all of us and all of them. Two years after passing Ken in the hallway, I made a promise to myself that I'd celebrate any additional degree I earned with a new tattoo. I scribbled designs during staff meetings, day-dreaming about the tattoo I'd get once I graduated from grad school. In grad school I counted on Mom, a proofreader by pro-fession, to check my essays and papers for grammatical mistakes. Even though she knew she was helping me and would be proud to hear my name called to receive my master's degree, the forty or sixty or hundred bucks I would offer her for working on my shit made us both content. And we both knew I needed her more than she needed me.

One night, she looked up from editing my latest paper. "Why are you always writing about being Black, Matthew? You're white too. You know that right?"

I had known this conversation would eventually come up. Every essay I composed, every topic I dove into, and every per-spective I took was a Black one. "I know, Mom," I responded. "It's just that ... it's just that ... you don't understand."

"I understand. I get it. But don't you ever think—"

"I do think about that," I said, cutting her off. "But when I step outside of this house, the world sees me as a Black man. And I see that the world sees me as a Black man. And when I look in the mirror, Mom ... You know."

She looked down at my paper on the dining room table and back up to me. "But you're also part white. You came from my body. You're part of me."

"I know, Mom. I know. You're right."

Mom returned her steely focus back to the pages. She didn't offer any comeback. None was needed.

"Thanks for helping me, Mom. I so much appreciate it. Love you," I said and walked around the table to kiss her on the top of her head.

"I know, I know," she said with only her eyes.

The last tattoo I got that Mom saw burned just like the first one had. After getting that degree that Mom helped me so much with, I almost couldn't wait to get home and show her. It was already dark outside when I rolled up to the front door. "Yo. Yooo? I'm home," I announced while closing the door behind me. "Pops, who's winning the game?" I didn't get a response. "Mom, Mom, what's up?" I let long seconds pass.

"Hey, Matt," she responded faintly. "I'm in the kitchen."

"Good. I got something to show you," I said. I was still living at home, a year older than the age Khaliff made it to, and my salary helped with the bills and confirmed that I'd escaped Black boyhood almost unscathed. And I had just gotten another step closer to defying what they thought about us. Another degree meant another piece of ink, another marker to inform them that I could look a certain way while existing and achieving in another way. It made me feel full inside and out. Confidence mixed with meagerness filled my insides as I stepped into the kitchen. "Mom, I got something for you."

"What?" she said weakly. She was leaning over the kitchen sink, not washing dishes, not eating food, just leaning. Just resting. I extended my left forearm out in front of her.

"Look," I said.

"What is it, Matthew?" Her voice had regained the power she had had back when she held my hand on our walks to and from grocery stores and parent-teacher interviews.

"It's a tattoo," I answered. "Take a look at it." It covered the top of my forearm. I had been a teacher for three years and I'd finally found the right image to commemorate my journey. An old-fashioned fisherman's tugboat was etched in simple black ink. A few fishing poles hung over the sides, razor-thin fishing lines dipping down into the black-inked waves below. Beneath the thick black waves were the words *He Eats Forever* in elaborate Old English capital letters. An image that perfectly captured my position in society as a teacher by invoking the proverb "Give a man a fish, he eats for a day. Teach a man to fish, he eats forever."

She studied my tattoo while I studied her thinning face. Her son had evolved. From a boy who tried to gel his hair and asked for frosted tips to a boy who buzzed his head and kept a one-level cut with a fade and a part in the front. To a teen who begged for an earring, then two, then fake diamond earrings, then a small tattoo. To a young man who asked for extra money to put gas in the blue Buick so that he could roll around with his seat tilted back and his left hand on the wheel. To a man who earned a degree and secured a good-paying job with benefits only to be mocked for the way he looked and the colour of his skin.

Her grey eyes gazed at the new image covering the skin on my left forearm. The new ink that commemorated a new achievement, a newer way of being me, the new pain I endured because covering up parts of my Black self seemed like the natural move the more I escaped what a nigga born in the mid-'80s was supposed to be about.

She looked at the tattoo without asking any questions. She refrained from asking a question like, Why did I feel the need to endorse a stereotype about Black men that represented the worst of them? Of us. Of me. I had a simple answer for her if she had asked. I wanted to tell her that I was now a teacher, a professional, a middle-class citizen who paid his bills and desired that decent middle-class lifestyle with a nice car parked on a nice driveway beside a nice home with a nice white picket fence around some nice green grass. Maybe my tattoos would allow the people outside to peek through the curtains and see that Black men with tattoos aren't just rappers and athletes and criminals and niggas. Some of them are teachers too. Being a nigga was part psychological and part aesthetic. I clung to my culture just like Ronnie Reed and David Stone clung to theirs. Ultimately, tattoos or not, I was a nigga but I was also just Matthew.

She didn't ask the question because she already knew the answer. I didn't ask either; I didn't ask for permission to get this tattoo, because I didn't need it anymore. "Did you notice anything, Mom?" My eyes searched hers, looking for a glimmer of appreciation.

"What am I supposed to notice? There's so much detail, son," she answered, exhausted by every word she uttered.

"The boat. Look right here. Look what it says," I said.

I directed Mom's grey eyes to the name on the stern of the boat: *Erna*. Mom's name.

Her eyes zoomed in on the four letters. *Erna*. It felt like we were the only people in the entire world. I wished I could crawl into her brain and know exactly what she was thinking.

"It's lovely, Matt. You got my name right there. It looks pretty. Nice, Matt. Very nice."

I wanted to hug her, but I wasn't yet used to feeling how scarce certain muscles and meats on her body had become and were beginning to make her feel. She pushed herself off the counter, reached up to put her hand on my cheek, and gave me a kiss. "Thank you, Matthew."

"Welcome," I said. "I'll get you a better gift for Mother's Day, promise." We laughed together.

Despite not asking for permission, I felt that Mom had given me her approval. Approval to be the type of Black man I saw and vowed to embody aesthetically. Embody on the surface—which over time is what the lucky ones learn to compartmentalize—not internalize. I was fortunate enough not to get caught up in the mirror, in those reflections they feed us through TV screens that depict the worst of Black folk. I was as lucky as the Ken Griffey Jrs., Will Smiths, and Puff Daddys were. As lucky as the unnamed Black men who looked, dressed, walked, and talked like Black culture but didn't get destroyed by what some people *outside* Black culture thought it meant.

A form of liberation arises in the space in which we create our own aesthetic. Where we decide what to wear on our bodies and how to walk and whether we'll pierce our ears and tattoo our skin. Our liberation arises when we are uniquely ourselves. Even when that means replicating superficial aspects of those who came before us. Construction of identity begins when we feel that first omission, that first taste of non-belonging, our learned reality. But then those constructions and coverings through non-belonging get consumed and interpreted in ways that solder all of us to each other, in a category, for better or worse. When others showed me that I couldn't escape the binding clasps of my Blackness, or the type of nigga I always wanted to be, my mom showed me something different. That night in the kitchen, Mom acknowledged my new tattoo on my forearm and told me it was okay—that I could be a nigga and be Matthew too.

MIXED THOUGHTS

My brother can do things I can't. Like hearing a door open when he's half-asleep or accurately eyeballing the weight of sized amounts down to the gram. Even though he earned his high school GED from Joyceville Institution, a multi-level prison 250 kilometres from home, his intelligence—about things that cannot be read about in books—far surpasses mine. Sometimes I think we grew up in two different worlds.

We got separate bedrooms when we moved into our house off Markham and Lawrence in the summer of 1991. "It's only fair," Mom explained, "that Matthew gets to pick which bedroom he wants. He's oldest." I could tell that Daniel was agitated, but at six years old, his feelings held no weight for me. Neither of us had control over our circumstances. At that time we were just kids living in Scarborough. We were told where to go, what to eat, and what time to come inside for bed. We didn't even know what *control* meant.

We were lucky our parents moved into a pocket of Scarborough that was still turning over its demographical leaves—the friends we made on our street were second-generation white Canadians and first-generation everything else. We were the two light-skinned "half-breed" brothers, close enough in age to have each other's backs and fend off any physical squabbles with outsiders. We were old enough to venture off on our own paths but young enough to be oblivious about what it meant to be Black kids; we didn't yet understand the economic factors that limited our ability to try. At that age, we only knew about fun and games. When the neighbours' kids invited us to play road hockey, grounders at the closest park, and cops and robbers on autumn evenings after the sun went down just before the street lights came on, we went. And we didn't come home until Mom shouted our names from the front steps. We knew nothing about what our skin meant. Beyond our separate bedrooms, we shared almost everything else.

I don't know about Daniel, but I started developing self-control and discipline around grade four. That's when I grew patient enough to accept my punishment and sit alone in the kitchen for an hour because I refused to eat overcooked green beans or the last bite of a well-done pork chop. That discipline, the control to withstand punishment, came from Mom and her hard-scrabble Jewish Polish upbringing in the late 1950s and early '60s when there wasn't enough matzah ball soup to go around. After sitting by myself a few nights while Mom went to the bedroom to watch murder mysteries and Pops slumped on the living room couch to watch whatever Toronto team was on television, I figured out that Dad felt just like Mom. He wanted me to remain seated until I finished those nasty-ass canned vegetables too.

Pops used fewer words but got his point across when he described how he grew up with twelve brothers and sisters who were all hungry when he was a kid "back a yard." If he ever dared to get up and leave his plate unattended, all his food would be eaten before he returned because "anything stay too long serve two masta." The idea of eating food off Daniel's plate made me queasy—his saliva might be on it—even if it was an extra cheesy bowl of Kraft Dinner. Tiny always ate all his food, anyways.

Despite my parents bringing their unique brand of love and care into our home, my brother and I couldn't fully identify with their experiences. I pictured the worlds my parents came from, and I knew that my brother and I were living in a different one. I was never Black enough to see myself in my dad's stories of his Jamaican upbringing and not even close to white enough to absorb my mother's experiences. My parents grew up in different environments, and the stories they told about their childhoods, in hopes of guiding me and my brother, were just that—stories.

The childhood Tiny and I shared was made up of different stories written in the margins. My predominantly white elementary school set me apart starting in the first grade. When Mom brought me to a parent-teacher meeting at the end of that first year at Golf Road Junior Public School and I asked her why, she said, "You know, I'm not quite sure why, Matthew. Ms. Owens told me that she wants to talk about the next school year." Knowing what I know now, she was being as honest and delicate as she could with me.

At the meeting, Ms. Owens talked about how I was falling below grade one standards and claimed I lacked an aptitude for remembering times tables in comparison to the other kids in her class. She suggested that I repeat the grade. I sat there quietly, her words immediately queuing up memories of spending time alone in her classroom after school filling out orangish-yellow worksheets that smelled like an overheated, inky photocopier and had big single digits on them. The six times tables had me sitting at my desk for an hour after school, just like Mom's green beans had me sitting alone at the kitchen table.

I was the only Black kid in that class. The only body that was ostensibly different. The only point of difference. Mom didn't even come close to verbalizing this with Ms. Owens. I listened to her talk with my white teacher about different expectations and how the school I previously attended had me finger-painting most days. Mom talked about expectations and opportunities. Opportunities and chances. Ms. Owens was stuck for words after Mom talked and defended and convinced. On the way home, she thrust her palm into mine, and after walking a block in silence said, "You need to learn how to defend yourself if you think things are unfair, Matthew." Whenever she used my name like that, it always made me think hard about her words. But back then, I didn't know what I was supposed to defend.

While Mom was protesting Ms. Owens's attempt to fail me in the first grade, Daniel was in junior kindergarten learning the alphabet song and how to count. In elementary school, we both learned to adore white things like hockey, Hanson, and hot dogs. By the time I got to middle school, our tastes changed along with the diversity among our classmates. Once we entered high school, our understanding of who we were was both influenced and supported by the friends we made, the things we enjoyed doing, and, of course, the things spoken and unspoken by our parents. Growing up Black, with a white mother and an immigrant Black father, living on the formerly Indigenous land we now call Scarborough, left me unsure of which parts of me I had to claim and which parts I had to defend.

The eighteen-month age difference between Tiny and me meant that I never spent significant time with him at school or in social circles beyond our street. He was two grades below me, so we didn't attend the same school for almost half of our scholastic careers. He never asked for help on homework, and when he was named valedictorian in grade six, I was envious. It was an accomplishment I hadn't earned and didn't even think about—until he had it. Years later, he told me that he was envious of my early success in sports and my later success with girls, and that his envy clouded the way he looked up to me. He realized that he would have to carve out his own path and develop his own identity. While I was trying to figure out who I was, he was doing the same thing.

Despite the social separation we experienced in our childhood, we lived under the same roof, spooned down the same dinners, and shared the same television, watching everything from cartoons to comedies to playing video games like *Mortal Kombat* and *NBA Live*. When family called, they were never able to tell the difference between our voices on the phone. Outside of family, most people found it hard to tell us apart.

Inside, though, we knew our differences. And at family gatherings, our aunts and uncles laughed about how much I'd inherited Pops' laid-back demeanour and Tiny had Mom's fiery nature.

Our innate dispositions separated us, as well as timing, circumstance, and affiliation. R&B and commercial hip-hop moved me. Tiny leaned toward the grittier side of rap and reggae. I got a job at Walmart because all my friends had started working part-time, plus I wanted to own more than one pair of shoes. Tiny somehow landed a job at a grocery store before he was old enough to be legally employed because he wanted money. No, he wanted to *hoard* money. My family hoarded all sorts of things, but money wasn't one of them. As teenagers, we had somewhat similar desires and formulated plans to fulfill them, but by the way we went about it, you'd think we were raised in two different families.

The lack of vacations, Power Ranger toys, and new Jordans motivated our desires and our competitive natures. We raced to the television on summer mornings to claim the remote control and were even willing to come to blows over it. As young teens, we didn't control much beyond that. Though we were venturing down diverging paths, we still had to share the TV in the living room, our parents' expectations about homework, and how long we could stay out. I think we shared a want for a lot of the same things. But we didn't share our thinking about the ways we could get what we wanted.

Near the end of high school, I moved to Ohio to follow my dream of playing pro football. At the time, I was worried more about how my absence would affect Pops than how it would impact my brother. When my high school girlfriend and I loaded my duffle bags and discounted three-drawer Walmart storage towers into her Toyota Echo, my brother, Dad, and Mom waved goodbye to me from the driveway. Dad, so overcome with pride and loss—and maybe a bit of beer and brandy—pissed his brown khakis. I slumped my head into my hands after waving in hopes that my tears would stop if I looked away from the ones dripping down Dad's cheeks. In that moment I didn't notice that by moving forward with my own life, I was leaving my little brother alone in his.

Although time, circumstance, and affiliation began to mature me, I wasn't prepared for the stories that I heard upon visiting home months later. Tiny told me first. He no longer bagged broccoli and herded carts outside the grocery store. He told me he quit because he made more money selling weed to his friends and high school peers in between classes. About $80 more a week. The risk he was taking didn't even factor into the meagre rewards; it was simple math. A skill he had learned early, won trophies for, and excelled at. A skill he was willing to use because the ends justified the means, bringing him opportunity, independence, and control. I could hardly come up with the words to argue with him because those same things held the same value for me.

While he talked about rap, friends, and fuck-ups, he rolled and smoked a blunt and I sipped on a glass of whisky. Dad walked in the kitchen and poured himself a shot and mentioned that the garbage bin needed to go down to the curb. Mom told us to turn down the music because it was getting late and she couldn't hear *Law & Order*. So Daniel lowered his voice and told me a story. About how he had been arrested with his friends for being in a stolen car. About how they tried to run, and how they thought they knew which way to turn and run but really didn't. About how he was bigger and Blacker than his friends, so when the cop chasing him got closer, he slowed. About how when the cop's screams of "Stop, stop!" got louder, Daniel did. He was out of breath anyways, he told me, laughing about it. He inhaled deeply on his blunt.

"Yo, I was in jail for two nights," he said, while looking up at me from the kitchen table. Half-smirking, half-ashamed, he exhaled weed smoke, looking at me for some sort of approval. I was hearing his entire story in parts. Small sections. Buzzing off the whisky I had been drinking, I said, "Damn. That's crazy." After a few moments of silence where we both awkwardly side-eyed each other, I asked, "Yo, you wanna play *NBA 2K*?"

The next time I came home, the stories he shared felt further away from the Daniel I knew. We had both eclipsed our teenage years and settled into our early twenties by striving toward goals with a common foundational desire: to make more out of our lot. Sports glory for me, money and independence for him. While I was learning how to be a man in a college dorm room in upstate New York, he was learning how to be a man in an apartment he rented twenty minutes from the childhood home he had outgrown, along with all its rules and expectations. Our ends justify our means. That was the subtext of our conversations, which on the surface were still about rap, friends, and fuck-ups. It was getting harder to find common ground. But at least then we could still touch each other and take for granted our presence in each other's lives.

After a while, Daniel stopped telling me stories, and I started to hear them from others. On a trip home after a year or so living in the States, I woke up at my girlfriend's house to an inordinate amount of missed calls and text messages on my Samsung flip. The first call I made was to my parents' house line.

Mom picked up and said, "Daniel's in jail. That idiot brother of yours. I told him to stop hanging out with those guys who sell weed and stay out all night. It's like they don't even have families." As her voice grew louder and more bitter, I wondered if she realized what she was doing: placing the blame for her son's mistakes on the boys he was hanging around with, without realizing that her and Pops' parenting style deserved some culpability. I wanted to ask her if she thought his independence, his moving out of their house after dropping out of high school, had played a role in his latest arrest. But I resisted, not wanting to press the topic over the phone. Especially after she said, "This time it's serious."

One of his boys stopped by the next morning to offer moral support to my parents and drop off some money for Tiny's jail canteen. He knew, at the time, what we didn't. That Tiny's stay in the Toronto East Detention Centre would be a lot longer than we hoped. "What the fuck is wrong with you guys?" Mom asked Chad. Despite being a close friend of Tiny's, Chad wasn't heavily involved in selling drugs, so Mom knew she could talk to him like that. Plus she liked him. Chad went to school with us, grew up playing basketball on the street, and had a part-time job in the auto department at Canadian Tire. His only infraction in my mother's eyes was that he smoked weed. Just like her husband and her youngest son. "I mean, honest to God. You guys are the stupidest fucking kids around. Smoking weed is one thing. But why do you idiots have to go out and sell it? I don't even know why you all smoke as much as you do. Now look at him. When the fuck are you all going to grow up?" Her verbal shots sprayed everywhere. And Chad, knowing Mom as long as he had, knew not to take the hits personally.

"I know, Moms, ugh. I don't know," he said, as I eyed him and nodded toward the front door so we could go outside and avoid her pain and disappointment.

"I mean, why can't he be like me and your dad? Like *your* parents, Chad? Get a decent job. Save some money. Live a regular life. Fucking Scarborough. We should have never moved here." She continued talking after we closed the screen door behind us. She didn't need us as an audience; her words fell on Pops' ears while he stared out the window, sipping brandy from his tea cup and lighting another cigarette.

"Yo, so what happened?" I asked. I had been at school in America for two years and the time away had loosened the bonds I shared with neighbourhood friends like Chad. My evolving Black masculinity was shaped by collegiate sports and American culture while Tiny's growth was impacted by the hazy purposelessness of broke, Brown, and Black Scarborough. My acculturation into spaces in Ohio and upstate New York was even stripping away my Scarborough accent. I'm sure Tiny's friends picked up on these subtle differences, but they didn't mention them. They understood how close me and my brother were and how lightly they had to step around that.

"Yo, so, we were on road yesterday, seen." Chad's strong Scarborough accent was tinged by his Jamaican roots; it made me miss being at home with the boys I'd become brothers with in high school. "And I guess the boy Tiney was under investigation, because next ting I know, tree undies plus a marked car boxed us in. I was going to rev it but, brother, der was no way outta dat."

I slowly shook my head and used my palm to wipe the sweat from my moustache. Chad must have known that I already knew he was in the car with him. And that I wanted to make sure that the other things Tiny's other boys told me the day before were true too. So I didn't even bother feigning surprise with a rhetorical question like, "Oh, say word, you were with him?" A question that would have demonstrated a lack of emotional distress on my part and de-emphasized the fact that I considered him a solid, stand-up, street-typa nigga.

But I needed the truth. I needed to process exactly what happened to my little brother, so I asked point-blank, "So where was the .38?" That question pushed our conversation to the point where it hit bone. I needed Chad to know that despite the physical distance between my brother and me, I still knew certain things about Tiny's interior life.

"Bro, he had it onnn him, fam. And I tink he had an eight ball in his boxers too." Chad took a gamble on divulging the entire truth to me, but I already knew the math didn't add up. Tiny'd been boasting about renting cars for days at a time, hotel rooms for his boys for the weekend, and paying our parents' bills; there was no way he was swinging all that with eighty extra bucks a week selling weed. I knew that my parents either didn't think about that or didn't want to believe it. Tiny was not selling weed. He was selling crack. And now he had been caught with some *and* a gun. And I was further away from him than I had ever been my entire life.

When I saw my brother next, we were seated about three feet apart with a half-inch-thick glass partition separating us. I picked up the phone and held it to my ear, checking his face for any signs of the prison melees I had seen in movies. "You alright, bro?" I knew that a holier-than-thou conversation would go nowhere and probably leave him feeling worse. Plus I was visiting with my parents and anticipated that Mom would have plenty of that for him once I gave her the phone.

"I'm good, bro. I fucked up. Had one more chop, and I was done for the night. Someone had to have snitched." His words were equally comforting and disappointing. He appeared to be unshaken, and I found it hard to admit to myself that that was what I most needed to see. But he was also naively defiant in the way he put the blame on others. Just like Mom had, days before.

In that prisoner visiting room, it was hard to process what was happening. I couldn't psychologically grapple with time and circumstance like I normally did. While he talked about that night's unfortunate events and gave me coded instructions on who to call and what to ask for, I found myself looking around. Watching a young Black mother cradle an infant on her lap while sterilizing the phone with wet wipes. Watching middle-aged white women who looked older than their years leaning toward the glass, laughing and joking and smiling with their partners, brothers, fathers sitting on the other side of the glass in orange jumpsuits, stroking long grey beards. Watching the constant shuttling of men on my brother's side of the glass, their eyes scanning the faces of every visitor before they found their designated stools.

"Yo?" my brother asked, his voice piercing through the phone a little sharper and louder. I fixed my eyes on him. "Are you listening?" he asked.

When I finally got to touch my brother again, it was a dim and chilly November afternoon in Scarborough. He had been sentenced to two years plus time served, and I was midway through my fourth year of school in the United States. I was only able to see him because his release date fell on American Thanksgiving and I had a brief break from classes. Somehow, the mental and physical separation we'd endured brought us closer. Prior to him coming out of jail, I'd gotten another tattoo on my back, this one depicting a paper-chain family that kids make in kindergarten. The words *Family First* were inscribed over the top and *One Love* inscribed below. I'd told him about it over the phone and couldn't wait to show him. Pops let me borrow his red Pontiac Aztek to go pick up Tiny and bring him home. Finally.

He walked out the sally port of the jail wearing slightly out-of-style clothes. A clear bag ballooning with personal items bounced off his thigh with each stride. When he noticed me, his smile extended from ear to ear, crinkling his eyes closed. I popped open the passenger door and turned the music up. "Free up, brother! How does it feel?" I asked.

"Ahhh. Blessed," he responded while exhaling deeply and looking to the back seat where he nodded and dapped Chad, who'd come along for the occasion. I wanted him to acculturate himself with his new environment so I played hip-hop songs I knew he would like: the latest tracks by less poppy and more gritty rap artists like Gorilla Zoe, Rich Boy, and Cassidy.

"Yo, Tiney," Chad hollered, then passed my brother a blunt. We headed home. Our home.

On the way there, we stopped at the LCBO and bought a bottle of Hennessy, popped into a convenience store to buy Tiny a pack of his favourite cigarettes and some chocolate bars, and ordered Pizza Pizza so that it'd be there shortly after we arrived. Finally having him back with us, surrounded by family and his closest friends, was reason to celebrate. Although his time in jail, during my time in U.S. colleges, made it feel unreal to be near him and made us love each other more, I felt like I had a lot of catching up to do. Like we both did.

I spent the rest of the afternoon swallowing double cognacs topped with Canada Dry while Tiny sipped shots between cigarettes and spliffs. The music blared while we took turns playing *NBA 2K* on our old PlayStation 2. I couldn't help but look over at my little brother every few minutes. To study him. To notice the changes to his body before anyone else did, including himself. I searched his face for signs of trauma and looked at his hair, his hands, his posture. I tried to remember what he looked and felt like before he went to jail. Before he decided to carry a loaded gun and sell crack cocaine. Before he decided that an hourly wage and high school courses weren't enough. But there was no difference. I couldn't put my finger on anything that diverged from the Tiny I'd known before. After a few hours of drinking, smoking, talking, and playing video games, Tiny fell asleep sitting up on the couch. I took the lit cigarette from between his fingers and put it out in the ashtray. I was satisfied that my little brother was home and already sleeping on the couch we used to fight over. Relieved that Tiny was still Daniel.

"How was Thanksgiv—ugh, how was your break, bro?" That's what my roommate, Tre, asked when I got back to college.

"Good. It was nice. My bro got out. Did a lil party. The man is finally free," I told him. Among the new friends I made in college, my Blackness was never in question. We all existed as outsiders at Colgate University, Black boys who did well enough athletically and academically to earn acceptance onto a lily-white liberal arts campus. Most of my closest friends in the two years I spent at Colgate arrived at the same time as me—for an initiation program we attended together the summer before our freshman year. They told the group—about twenty or so of us—that the program would help us get used to the academic rigour of college and familiarize ourselves with the campus. It just so happened that, unlike the majority of students who enrolled there, each person in this summer "institute" was from an inner city. I met boys from Atlanta, Chicago, Queens, D.C., and Dallas. I didn't know if I was included in this program because I was Canadian or because they had somehow heard about Scarborough.

While the fact of my Blackness was never really in question, its degree was. Summer camp peers from notorious parts of America who quickly became teammates, roommates, and boys gently chided me when I asked where the *washroom* was, or for one of them to give me a *drive* up the hill to class. When I told Tre to phone me when his basketball practice was over, my other boys laughed. *Phone* sounded foreign and odd to my American boys. "Yeah, Tre, why don't you ring me on the ol' telly when you're done," Jude cracked. "It's *call* me, you damn Canadian." In college, my Blackness was compromised by my nationality or my accent and diction, both of which were beyond my control. I didn't know which one created the gap I felt between me and my American boys at times. Either way, I had a familial story I could wield to shore up any deficiencies they found in my Canadian Blackness.

"Oh, word," Tre said after I told him about my Thanksgiving-without-the-turkey back in Canada on November break. "Damn, he was down for a minute. Tell him I said welcome home next time y'all talk." My boys at school all knew about Tiny. Eventually. At first I didn't share his story with any of them. I felt a bit ashamed and embarrassed. Vaguely vulnerable. I was starting to understand my own Blackness in the American context, the context I thought I already fully understood through watching movies, visiting relatives, and listening to hip-hop for the previous decade and a half. And I was hesitant about throwing an added layer into that fog when I was still learning basic colloquialisms.

"For sure. I really hope he stays straight after this. You know, wake up and do something with his life. 'Cause jail ain't no joke, bro."

"I know," Tre answered. Neither of us had been to jail before.

Sharing Tiny's story with my boys filled in parts of my Blackness that I could have never supplied myself. That I felt I'd never needed to. I had sports for that. And parts of school for that. I bought clothes for that. And mimicked hip-hop for that. And while Daniel played the same sports on the street, had the same teachers at school, and watched the same shows on television at home, I think he must have felt like there was something missing. My brother and I were only eighteen months apart in age and lived under the same roof for eighteen years; we were searching for the same thing but seeking it in different ways. That thing we both pursued made him make decisions that squeezed out all the bits of Blackness inside of him. Or maybe it wasn't the Blackness that forced him to do that.

The pieces of Blackness that I picked up throughout my childhood and teenage years in Scarborough were underscored by my time away from it. I held onto the pieces I was willing to redeem. That made the decision to return home to finish my undergrad straightforward. I moved back and settled into my parents' basement. I got a part-time job at the local Goodlife Fitness and spent the rest of my time training for football and lifting weights, studying and attending class, and hanging out with my old boys from high school. Even though I was back at home, I barely saw my brother. He was living in his new apartment, hanging out with his friends, working until sun-up, then sleeping in until two or three in the afternoon.

The times he stopped by the house felt ceremonial. He'd pull up in a shiny Corvette or brand-new Escalade, carrying bags of groceries or a brand-new flat-screen television, or with bundles of scratch tickets. After ordering mountains of food for us while he juggled calls on three different phones, he'd get up, kiss Mom on the forehead, and tell Dad that he'd be back in a few days. Every time before leaving, he'd pull out a lump of freshly creased bills, count a flurry of them off, and leave the counted stack on the same old splintered living room table where we ate bowls of cereal in front of the TV as kids. My parents acted weird about that money. For a couple hours, they would pretend it wasn't there. After some time had passed and the conversation changed, one of them would pick it up and count it and carry it away, stuffing it into an envelope that held money from the last time he stopped by.

I finished college and got a job teaching at an elementary school that was only a twenty-minute drive from my parents' basement. It was the first time I was earning real money. The type of money that made me feel like a man. The school board paid me a salary and benefits. And I still worked as a personal trainer at a boutique fitness club in downtown Toronto, blocks away from where my parents first met each other thirty years earlier. I was working from morning to night at two different jobs and cleared close to $100,000, almost double what both my parents made. Buying multiple pairs of shoes no longer satisfied me, so instead I splurged on a brand-new BMW 3 series. The monthly payments dented my chequing account but it was a price I was willing to pay to look and feel like the nigga I'd always wanted to be. I took pride sitting in the driver's seat every time I unlocked the car doors for friends. I finally felt like I had the ammo to pull up to my brother's apartment. Like I finally had the wisdom to talk to him on the level that we'd always been looking to talk to each other on.

"Bro. You can't do this forever." I'd waited until most of his friends had left, and he'd turned down the music just a little bit. "Like, bro, there really is no point where you come out on top, bro. Think about it. Think, bro." I made sure I was looking him dead in the eyes. "Tiny, think about it . . ."

"Think about what?" he asked, slumping back into a brown leather La-Z-Boy across from me. "Bro, my program is tight. I'm not out here on some waste movements. I'm different, G." He tapped the bottom of his cigarette pack and pulled out a smoke. "You think I'm stupid?" He lit his cigarette and laughed loud. "You think I'm stupid, eh?"

"Bro, I know you're not stupid. Look around. You're good. What I'm saying is that the money you make comes with chances. Serious chances. And why take them? You're already good. You can make the same amount of money doing something legit." He watched me while I took another sip of my drink. "Bro, ballpark it. How much money do you even make a week?" I was ready to finally be his big brother and tell him the things I'd learned. Things I learned about being a man, being Black, being from Scarborough. "How much would you say you make a week?" I asked again, not giving him time to answer. Hoping that he would feel the pressure, see the success I'd achieved *outside* the stereotypical ways to exist as a Black man.

"A week?" he asked. He bent down in his recliner and closed his eyes tight. It was late and we were both a bit drained. Then he tilted back, looking at the ceiling with his eyes open, counting in his head. I waited for his answer, frustrated that Ms. Owens and those six times tables popped into my memory, along with my little brother's gold valedictorian trophy sitting on the dresser in the upstairs room that Mom now slept in.

"All the hours you have to put in, all the money you have to spend on it. Think about it, bro. C'mon, you don't make that much at the end of a week. How much would you say you make after all that?" I was counting on a certain amount, counting on the fact that when he finally admitted it to me, I could really give it to him. Prove that his path was futile, stupid, hopeless, while the path that I took was righteous, meaningful, appropriate. Prove that Scarborough made him learn and relearn a form of Blackness that I had escaped. Prove that our parents were right in how they raised us.

He opened his eyes and took another draw of his cigarette. "A week? Probably ten racks." Then he stared at me, half-smirking, half-ashamed, almost as if he was looking for me to answer with something better and bigger and Blacker than that. "Yeah, probably ten thousand." He looked vulnerable and meagre. But he looked me straight in my eyes. It was the first time I had seen my brother in a long time.

I stared back at him. The only thing I could say back to him was "True?"

True.

My expectation blew up in my face. I scrambled to make sense of what he'd said so matter-of-factly. And because I couldn't find words to articulate the love and fear I felt for him cooking up and breaking down crack rock on a weekly basis, I said nothing. Because like him, I pursued a particular dream of Black manliness. Even though I had a job as a teacher, I was still trying to become a professional football player. By doing so, I put my body in danger. And how was that different from what he was doing? Both our understandings of what it meant to be a Black man were still in process. I sat there staring at my brother. In awe of how he'd manufactured and then navigated his own success, and in shock at his willingness to follow through on it. I was too tired to ask if he wanted to play video games.

———

Late November was a distant memory by the time my brother told me that he wasn't coming to my girlfriend's parents' house for Easter dinner. "I'm busy today, bro. EI cheques just cashed. Feigns got extra money to burn on statutory holidays." I had had a feeling he wouldn't want to spend hours with a family he'd met only a few times anyway. Why sit around playing card games and talking about shit that was irrelevant to him? "I'm at the crib. They're getting ready. I'll drop Moms and Pop close to where you're at."

We settled on a Shoppers Drug Mart on Queen Street East, near the basement apartment I lived in with my girl. It was a straight drive for him down the Don Valley Parkway. I heard him before I saw him. "I know, I know. I'm late. Fuck, they take forever just to close the door and get in the car. Like, the house isn't going to burn down. The stove was off the first time you checked it." Tiny's tone was hot and condescending enough to let everyone know that he thought he was doing us all a favour by being there. "I'm not coming back to pick them up. I got shit to do. Already killed off half my day."

My parents got out of the back seat of his pearl-white Escalade and hopped into the backseat of my BMW, my girlfriend in the front passenger seat. "We're like three minutes away. I'll give y'all a ride back home. Don't worry," I said. I left the parking lot and cruised down a few side streets before I slowly pushed the brake pedal and put the car into park. I didn't hear the knock on my window when I pulled the keys out of the ignition. The second knock exploded through my senses when I went to open my door. A man standing outside my car window had a Glock pointed at my head. It wasn't a .38 revolver or a sawed-off shotgun; I had seen those before. The man with the Glock pointed at my face was yelling things I couldn't hear. I was frozen. He yanked open my door.

"Get out the car! Get out the car!" he screamed. I unbuckled my seat belt and did what I was told.

"Hands on the car! Hands on the car!" the guy with the gun yelled.

I followed his instructions. All my energy was devoted to following this man's orders while trying to decipher what was happening to me. My brain and my body felt stuck. I was outside the car with my hands on the hood when another man with a gun drawn swooped toward the passenger side doors. He directed my girlfriend and parents out of the car. This seemed to be taking too long, the men moving too tactically for it to be a robbery or carjacking. I noticed that two cars had boxed in mine—one had pulled up behind me and another one was adjacent to my door.

The man who had first knocked on my window started patting me down and said, "Give me your ID." I focused on his hand with the gun. It was slightly shaking. For some reason, that made me both nervous and relieved.

"It's in my wallet. My wallet is in the car. I'll get it," I told him. On the street, a few front doors opened. I sent a silent prayer to God that my girlfriend's parents not be among the neighbours who had peeked out to see what all the yelling was about.

"No," the man shouted. With a gun in his hand, he said, "Tell me where your wallet is in the car and I'll get it."

It was all starting to make sense to me. The guns, the barking orders, the white men in flannel shirts and Oakley sunglasses and ball caps and blue jeans and laced-up workboots. The black-lettered commercial plates on the two Toyota Camrys. While everyone else was travelling to their Easter festivities, these men were working, just like my brother. Except these men were the cops.

"You need a warrant to go in my car. And the trunk too," I said. I knew that I had minimal leverage in this situation and wanted things to end as quickly as possible, but I felt a touch resistant. Besides stealing a few chocolate bars and chips back in middle school, I had done nothing to warrant this treatment, this infraction of my freedoms. This violation of my body. I had done everything right. Everything, more or less, that I was told to do. I'd gone to school, graduated, got a job, paid taxes, spent time with family on holidays like Easter. And now I was standing with my hands on the hood of the car I worked hard to buy, with a gun pointed at my face. I was being told that I couldn't get my own wallet to prove who I was.

"The guy who you probably followed from Scarborough to the Shoppers Drug Mart? That's my brother. He was dropping off our parents so we can go celebrate Easter. That's all that *drop-off* was, bud. You got the wrong guy." I instantly regretted opening my mouth, knowing that I'd eventually have to tell my brother what I'd told these undercovers. But I wanted them to understand that my brother and I were two different people living in two separate worlds. That even though we shared the same fixed address and parents, parts of those deep connections had long been split apart. After handing my driver's licence to another undercover, the cop with the gun went back to his Camry and huddled with his partners. A few minutes later they handed back my licence and got into their cars. Without saying anything else to me, my parents, or my girlfriend, they drove off.

The next day I told my brother what happened. He'd already heard the story from Mom, and I could tell by his reaction that her understanding of what took place wasn't as full as mine. She'd lamented about the unfairness of stereotypes and police profiling when I told her about recent times I'd been pulled over in my new BMW for no apparent reason and been sent on my way with no ticket. She thought that the Easter episode was another one of those situations. "So what'd they say?" Tiny asked.

"Nigga. They didn't *say* shit! They damn near took off the front of my whip and hopped out with their guns, yelling for me to get out," I answered. He laughed. "I told them that whoever they were looking for, they pulled over the wrong guy. Told them I'm your brother, not your plug."

"Nah, you didn't say that, did you?"

I knew why they'd pulled us over. The undercovers knew who he was and were watching him. They wouldn't have stopped us and drawn guns on us if he wasn't under some type of police investigation. His question suggested that he didn't want to accept this fact. "Yeah, bro. I did. Fuck them."

I stopped myself from plunging into a diatribe about how fucked it was that his actions were now impacting me and our parents and how, when I thought about it, they had been for years. How, if he put his mind to it, he could go get a job somewhere; with his skill and his intelligence and his leadership qualities, he could be a boss in some corporate office just like how he was a so-called boss on the streets. How the jobs that he could eventually get might earn him almost as much as he was making out there now, with benefits. And how he wouldn't have to look over his shoulder every time he got in his car, and if he did get pulled over, like I got pulled over, he could tell the cops no without worrying because he'd be good and clean, just another Black guy pulled over for no reason by the cops. And fuck them anyways because, like everyone else, they looked at Black guys as if we were all the same, so why not be more like me and play the game they wanted us to play but do it safer, instead of letting them win?

Instead I just stared at him.

"You're right. Fuck 'em," he said. "Let's go downstairs and watch a movie."

Less than a year later, Tiny was arrested again. This time he didn't get caught running away from a stolen car or driving down some road late at night with a gun and crack on him. He was arrested in the parking garage at his own place, where he'd lived since moving out of our childhood home, five kilometres away. He didn't have a gun on him or any drugs. They found those things inside his apartment after showing him a search warrant and using his own keys to open the door. This time he wasn't going to the East Toronto Detention Centre for a few days or a few months. They booked him downtown at the Don Jail; after he signed off on a plea bargain, they sent him to a prison outside of Kingston, Ontario, called Joyceville Institution to serve his sentence. Possession of a controlled substance with the intent to sell, along with a few counts of possession of a prohibited weapon—this time "for a dangerous purpose" due to his prior convictions. He was sentenced to eight to ten years, with the possibility of parole in who knows when. None of us—my mom, my dad, or I—could recall the number after we heard the judge lay down his prison time.

Tiny hadn't yet turned twenty-five and would be celebrating his next birthday as a convicted felon. A little over eighteen months earlier, I had celebrated mine as a freshly minted elementary schoolteacher. Looking at him in the prisoner's box, I wondered how the races to the couch in our living room, the ball hockey on the street, and the decision to mix in green beans with mashed potatoes so we could get up from the dinner table had affected our outcomes. That day in court was the last time I laid eyes on my little brother for a few years.

Back in college, telling Tiny's story to my boys helped cement my Blackness. I would have survived without telling it, and Daniel actually had to live it. I guess the lifestyle made him feel whole. From the prisoner's box, he looked at me and nodded with a half smirk on his face. With my throat getting tighter and tighter, I nodded back and balled a fist over my chest. I made a silent prayer that he'd be able to come to terms with his decisions. And that the years away from our parents, friends, and our home wouldn't change him. Just like how they didn't change me.

SIX P.M. IN TORONTO

CHAPTER 8

Aunt Mavis used to say that late on the night her son, Khaliff, died, she heard the side door to the house open and footsteps go downstairs to Khaliff's basement space and bedroom. Our whole family knew that he had left home that day at dusk to confront a lingering situation and never returned to their house in Oak Park, succumbing to stab wounds in the back of an ambulance on the way to DMC Sinai Grace. But she swore that before, or right after, he passed that night, he had *come home*.

At eighteen, the thought of my favourite cousin, the man I idolized, no longer existing, left me disoriented. I didn't understand how a death can dismantle your understanding of living. Bits of my heart and brain broke off into an inner dark abyss. I had graduated high school and skipped out on graduation and the post-factum homecoming months later. Despite the reverence I felt for Khaliff and what he meant to my growth as a Black boy, I found it necessary to push forward. At eighteen, I couldn't wait to *leave* home.

I was in search of things—experiences, friends, moments—that would prove my existence worthwhile. I chased a Black Americanness that would at least leave me with an adopted accent and the ability to play a sport better than my friends back home. Another part of me wanted to leave Scarborough—leave Canada—because my father had left Jamaica. *For a better life.* When he told his tales about a time before he met Mom, when he landed in a foreign country, my father beamed with energy and pure contentment. To become fully satisfied with myself, I figured I had to go away too. To know myself meant leaving behind the things that made me.

When I eventually returned home at twenty-two, I was changed, I thought. Changed in a way that Mom and Dad didn't acknowledge but still somehow knew. They knew that I had become someone different, closer to the picture I'd painted deep in my recesses.

A man, I thought.

I thought I had been gone long enough to render myself grown. I thought I no longer depended on their support. I had no idea how malleable that word, *support*, would become. How my idea of it would be bent and moulded to mean *time* or *safety* or *love*. When I heard Aunt Mavis tell people how her son came back home as he died, I didn't understand how the words we use to describe our lives bow outside our flesh. Outside our breath. I had yet to grasp how those words—*support, time, safety, love,* and *home*—travel through time and space to create our reality.

Mom was upset when she came downstairs and saw five black garbage bags lined up near the bottom of the steps. "What is all this, Matthew?" she asked. "You can't just throw out all of my old things. All of our old things."

"You're a hoarder, Mom," I replied. "Most of this shit was sitting in these closets before I even left for college. Shit, and a lot of the stuff is from when me and Tiny still used the basement as a playroom." I gripped two bags and hefted them up the stairs.

"My old clothes," she called out. "Matthew, what the fuck? These are my old clothes. Some expensive stuff is in those bags. What the fuck are you doing?" She pulled two linen dresses from a bag, fixed the hangers back to the shoulder straps, and walked toward the closet in the basement space that I was trying to make my own.

"Mom. Are you serious right now? I've actually never in my life seen you wear those dresses. You don't even wear dresses. C'mon, I'm trying to clean up." It had been years since I had needed to persuade Mom to do something for me. Our conversations had evolved onto topics like jobs after college, marriage, and kids, while occasionally reverting back to spending habits and dirty dishes and four eggs for breakfast instead of two.

"You're throwing away memories, asshole."

I grabbed the dresses and shoved them back in one of the garbage bags. I didn't even look at her when I said, "I'm throwing away *clothes*, Mom. Old clothes."

When you're in your early twenties, with a college degree, a decent-paying job, and a background that doesn't match your parents, you begin to think that you don't need Mom and Dad anymore. And you begin to think that they don't need you. That's what I thought after coming home from the States.

Although I was still living at home, my parents became invisible to me. It had been at least a decade since we sat together at the kitchen table for dinner and at least five years since I asked permission for anything. I had been moving forward in life, eagerly anticipating weekends with friends, nights out with my boys, and vacations planned months in advance.

On a weekly basis, aunts, uncles, cousins, and older friends told me that *kids* in their twenties—kids like me—thought they were invincible. I'd look stonily into their eyes and think, Yes, you're right. I do think I'm invincible.

I had a question ready to respond to their blithe gospel, albeit one that I never spoke aloud: "You ever see a Black Superman? No? Well, you're looking at one." I can't account for my attitude except to say that in my early twenties time seemed to move at my will. I only learned about the fluidity of time years later, when it stopped.

———

I was on the patio of a club on Queen Street East and I didn't hear my phone ring. The music inside was too loud, and I had a propensity to not check voicemails until days later. My former manager at Walmart was trying to branch out and was holding a launch party for his new clothing line. I'd stopped by early to help him set up and was taking a break when I noticed my house number light up the screen on my Samsung flip.

"What's up? I'm busy," I answered, before anyone on the other end could get a word in.

"Matthew, it's me. Are you alone?" Those words, to Black supermen my age, didn't necessitate pause.

"It's Thursday afternoon, Mom. No, I'm not alone. I'll be home later on though. Probably around eleven." I thought my brisk response would get her off the phone.

"Your dad has prostate cancer. The doctor says he has prostate cancer." She spoke so matter-of-factly I almost felt like I had been disrespected.

"What the fuck are you talking about?" I asked, ashamed that I couldn't formulate a better reply that expressed how my stomach had dropped. In that second after responding, I wished I was Superman enough to rewind time a little.

"Cancer," she repeated. "Hopefully it isn't that serious." Hearing her speak that word through my phone made me feel invisible. "What time are you coming home? No rush. Just asking."

He was in and out of the hospital in a matter of days. According to his doctor, a handful of pills mixed with small doses of targeted therapy would shrink the tumour growing on his prostate. Apparently, my grandfather also had this affliction; it runs in the family without respite, I was told later. But when Dad was diagnosed, I was still too caught up in building my own life to consider how my hereditary disposition could affect me.

"Water, Gatorade, lots of rest, no strenuous activity. Got it. Anything I'm missing, doctor?" I was proud that I didn't have to ask him what the word *strenuous* meant.

When the doctor checked his clipboard and shook his head, I replied, "Cool. I'll stop at the grocery store tomorrow." I turned to Mom. "Maybe we'll go after I get home from work."

On the drive home, I mentally mapped out how I would fit grocery shopping with Mom into my Tuesday. Pops was in his late fifties when he got cancer, still drinking liquor like a fish, cooking dinner, too, and him dying didn't seem possible, so I wasn't emotional about any of it.

To start that college football season, I bought a new pair of cleats and used a navy-blue Sharpie to write *for my dad* on the heel of both shoes. I drew a heart at the end of the phrase. When people asked about the inscription, I told them that I was dedicating the season—my last one as a college athlete—to my dad, who had been recently diagnosed with cancer. I used his cancer to give my last season more meaning. I used his suffering selfishly. I can't explain it, but I knew he wasn't going to die from cancer. I mean, I didn't know. But I *knew*, in my bones, that he would survive. I had been gone from him too long for him to just become invisible like that. And the world still revolved around me.

On the night of our season opener, Tucker agreed to drive over to my house and get a ride to my football game with my parents. I was ready to show my true self to my family and closest friend. The me that I had curated and chiselled down to its most notable parts: athlete by way of the platform I learned to thrive on, entertainer by virtue of seeking attention through established modes of performance, criminal by means of leveraging intimidation for the sake of personal advantage. The day before, I begged the sports information director at the University of Toronto for an extra five tickets and told her, "These extra tickets gonna guarantee us a win. You don't know what it's like when family comes to a game. I played ball in the States. And even back in Scarborough, when family comes, it's different." She handed me a roll of seven tickets and wished me good luck. Better than most, she knew our home games only ever had a few hundred people in the stands. "Thank you. Make sure you're there tomorrow too. Front row," I added. "I'll point to you *when* I score a touchdown."

Whenever Mom and Dad came to a game, they sat in the same place, making it easy for me to spot them. That night I couldn't. Every couple of minutes, I would look up into the barren bleachers at Varsity Stadium and scan for Mom's face or listen for Dad's signature "Go, Matthew!" scream that I'd heard since I was four years old.

I heard and saw nothing.

Three hours later, after the game ended, when no family greeted me under the grand stanchion, I undressed, showered, changed into my sweatsuit, and caught the Bloor subway line heading east. Heading home.

Mom was asleep in front of the TV, and Pops was upstairs in bed snoring with a cigarette burning a hole through his pillow. Only the bathroom light was left on. I turned it off and headed downstairs to my basement space.

"We got into an accident on the 401 last night," Mom told me the next morning, after asking why I needed to scramble three eggs when two with a little more milk would yield just as much. I didn't even look up from my plate. "Fucking guy can't stop after one beer," she went on. We both knew that when she said one beer, she meant two. We both knew that two meant six. She stirred cream into her coffee and whispered, "Thank God we're alive."

Mom was always reluctant to dole out thank yous, so I could tell she really meant it. Usually her eyes spoke. She was built like me. Rather, I was built like her. In addition to being stingy with thanks, I obsessively checked my pockets like she checked light switches. I lost my house key at a 7-Eleven in grade eight, and since then I'd been double-checking my jean pockets, theatre floors, and every seat I sat on after getting up. In ninth grade I unlocked the front door to my house and dodged my dad swinging his belt yelling, "You damn fool. Coulda burnt the whole house down." After shelling up and taking welts, I made sure the stove top was always off before rushing away to school.

Mom used to frustrate Tiny and me when she would pick lint off the floor right in front of the television, forcing us to pause our PlayStation game and squawk that she was in front of the screen. "It's your mess that I'm picking up," she'd reply. We thought she was picking at the carpet out of spite because we left the ketchup on the kitchen counter or put the juice in the fridge without a cap. When I started turning my car engine off to go back in the house to make sure I'd closed the fridge, even though I knew that I'd closed it, I realized that parts of her would always be in me. Later on, that made me content. But back then, I never really thought to say thank you.

Instead, I looked at Mom's compulsive ways and Pops' mundane nightly regimen like they were a burden on me. So I moved out. Settling into a basement apartment in the Riverdale area of Toronto, near Broadview and Danforth. Another new beginning. This time, I hoped it would lead somewhere.

Away again, I recreated myself through a combination of osmosis and reflection. Trial and error. Me finding me, without the help of Mom and Dad, didn't last long. I'd learned to put the food away after eating, wash the dishes when the sink got full, and grocery shop before the butt ends of the bread loaf touched each other, but I hadn't learned those intrinsic, intangible lessons. I'd forgotten the lesson of buying a bag of marbles because others would be upset if they didn't get something, of holding hands to cross the street to express love as well as to show safety and strength. I'd forgotten the sound of my name in my mother's mouth, spoken with love or consternation, moving me forward in a better way. I'd forgotten all those lessons. I lost them when I tried to find myself on my own.

That's what made me come back home one more time. To learn things I couldn't pick up by myself. To finally solve the puzzle of being a young Black man. At least, that would have been a nicely wrapped up, full-circle, coming-of-age revelation. But the truth is the latest relationship I was in deteriorated, and I couldn't afford to pay the lease note on my BMW *and* rent my own apartment on my salary.

In my mid-twenties, the last place I wanted to live was in the basement of my parents' house. But the truth, like time, doesn't always align with our wishes.

On occasion, Pops would remind me that he had moved out of his parents' home in Jamaica at sixteen. The glorious stories he told about carving his own path faded into sobering lessons. Every few months, Pops would remind me that he left home because his father told him that "one house can't serve two masters." I didn't even catch a whiff of the patriarchal stench of his comment at twenty-five. Now I often wonder if his mom felt the same way. If she looked at her home as an institution meant to serve one (male) master. Mom definitely didn't look at it that way. She was the queen of her castle. And Pops' parables were meant more to be taken as guidance, not literal instruction. This was the same guy who pissed his pants and cried when I first left for America at nineteen. He liked his sons at home. Now he had one of them back under his roof for the foreseeable future. Mom too.

Time's funny like that. Only after it passes can you see what you were blind to in the moment.

Adjusting to living with my parents again was a process. Answering questions on my way out the door on a Friday night about where I was going and what time I was coming home felt demeaning. I reminded them that I was a grown-ass man. They reminded me that I lived in their house rent-free. I brought up all the groceries I was buying. They brought up all the dinners they were making. They told me to call if I was not coming home for the night. I left drunken messages at two in the morning.

Mom bought Dad birthday cards and signed them for me. I bought him a bottle and some scratch tickets. She ordered quarter chicken meals from Swiss Chalet. I paid the delivery man when he knocked on the door. Mom sang "Happy Birthday" to Pops over the steaming rotisserie chicken breast. I unenthusiastically chimed in. That's what we did on special occasions; most nights we made our own plates and hoped that Tiny would call. Mom would retire to her bedroom, Pops to the living room couch, me to the basement. Hours later, I'd run into Mom in the kitchen, filling up a cup with ice cream.

"What flavour?"

"Rocky Road," she'd answer.

"C'mon, Mom, you know I never liked Rocky Road."

"I bought this for me."

When my brother called from prison—which he did almost every day—Pops would carry most of the hour- to two-hour-long phone conversations. I didn't have much to say to my brother. Not because

I was disappointed or upset at him, but because there was nothing much to talk about.

"How's Mom and Dad?"

"Alright."

"How's work?"

"Same old."

"How are you doing?"

"Okay."

"What did you do on the weekend?"

"Same regular shit."

"What's the weather like over there?"

"Getting colder every day."

Talking with my brother was like talking with Mom and Pops every day. Nothing was different from one day to the next. Invisible in our own bodies until time, support, safety, love, home called on us to be present. There. And then we were. And we were all fine with it.

Time, and those other things, are funny like that.

I was proud of Mom. She had always talked about shedding her "pregnancy pounds" and getting back to the weight she'd been in her twenties. In her sixties she was finally doing it. When I was ten, my grandmother—Pops' mom—came to Canada for a visit. I marvelled at her long silky silver hair, her vibrant maroon-brown skin, and her healthy frame. Mom, Dad, Aunt Ena (who lived twenty minutes away in Pickering), and a few other Jamaican relatives whose names I can't remember sat on the porch at my parents' house.

My dad was happy; he hadn't seen his mother in twenty years. When my grandmother—whom I was meeting for the first time— was introduced to my mother, she gave her a big smile and hug and exclaimed, "Lordt, she fat, Neville." I never looked at my mom as big. *Fat* was outside the realm of identities I layered onto her.

Aside from my dad, she was the strongest person I knew. She could walk home from the grocery store carrying five to six bags on each hand without complaining. Her ability to carry me and then my brother, to bend and split and eventually burst back: that type of weight signified strength. Not anything else.

Dad and Aunt Ena and the rest of my Jamaican relatives chuckled and carried on talking about cold Canadian weather in the summer and the dutty apple trees growing in our backyard that weren't really apple trees. I got lost in the novelty of new-found family members demonstrating deep love through looks and words and proximity. So lost that after twenty minutes, I finally noticed that Mom wasn't outside with us.

I found her sitting alone at the kitchen table in the corner. She had both hands clasped around a cigarette. Her glasses and a crumpled Kleenex were beside the ashtray.

"Mom, what's wrong? Why are you crying?" I couldn't remember if I'd ever seen my mom cry before. I felt myself taking a step back in shock. "Mom, what's the matter?"

She mumbled words like *fat* and *disrespectful* and phrases like *coming into my own home* and *if it weren't for me, her son would be—*

"I think it's just her culture, Mom. Their culture. I don't think that word means the same thing it does here." I wanted to help Mom. To support her. My grandma seemed old and different. I wanted to go outside and shove my grandma to the ground and tell her that I hated her long grey-ass hair and her reddish-brown skin and her stupid Jamaican accent. She made my mom cry, and I wanted to make her feel the same weight. Instead I stood in the kitchen staring at my mom. "I'm gonna have some Rocky Road ice cream. You want me to make you a cup?"

We went to Winners so Mom could look for Christmas presents. It was early November, and although an old girlfriend and I had started to restore our broken relationship, I was still living at home, fully adjusted to living with my mom and dad. I'd actually started to enjoy it. I was approaching thirty, and for the first time in my life, my bank account was over four digits on a consistent basis, and Mom seemed better too. Her obsessive compulsiveness wasn't as bad.

She had entered her sixties and spent less time looking through identical cans of tuna and more time asking me if the jeans she was trying on were worth the price. And she needed new jeans. And new tops. The impending mass layoffs at her work had finally hit her—she was grappling with life as a quasi-retired, almost senior citizen. "Two more years and I'm going to be saving tons of money on toilet paper and all the other shit we need for the house at Shoppers Drug Mart, Matt. You know at sixty-five, you get a seniors' discount?"

"Okay, Mom," I laughed. "I don't know why you're telling *me* that because I got like thirty-plus years to get there. And when *you* do, Mom, I ain't driving you over to Shoppers ten times a week to save two bucks on some Kleenex and toothpaste."

"One day you'll understand," she said, her refrain every time I hinted at her frugality.

I always rolled my eyes at that. I was lucky to never have to think about time back then.

I watched her feed her peeling leather belt through the loops of her new better-fitting, slimmer jeans as she looked at herself in the mirror. I took notice of her determination as she drank coffee after coffee for breakfast and ate one or two yogurt cups for dinner. All she could stand, she said every now and then. In her sixties, Mom was no longer what her mother-in-law would consider fat. In fact, if my grandmother were back on the porch now, she would have probably said, "Lordt, she *skinny*, Neville," with the same benevolent matter-of-factness she used to describe Mom twenty years prior. I was proud of what she had accomplished, not in twenty years but in one. Mom became my model.

Time's funny like that. And other things too.

Her weight never concerned me until the new clothes she bought started to fit like the old ones. Those ones I'd sized up and thrown out. One day, after noticing that she didn't bother to eat a plate of Dad's barbecued chicken or her own baked potatoes, I asked, "Are you sure you're losing weight in a healthy way, Mom?"

"I eat. I just don't like how meat and stuff sits in my stomach anymore. I still eat vegetables, Matthew. And I drink milk . . . in my coffee at least." She laughed. "Your brother should get on a diet like me. He tells me he eats bully beef and fried rice. What the hell is bullied beef? That guy eats way too much garbage."

Dad and I regularly visited my brother at Joyceville Institution where he was serving the final years of his sentence. Mom didn't come. She was built like that. "He's made my hair grey enough. When he calls, I'll tell him what an asshole he was and what movies he's missing out on." Her way of talking about her youngest son put everyone at ease. If Mom could take it, we all ought to be able to. She sometimes carried more weight than us all.

"Yeah, when he gets out, you can show him how yogurt and coffee fill you up just as much as eggs for breakfast and chicken for dinner do," I joked. "And if you don't like your grey hair, they got hair salons for that, Mom. They got shit these days that damn near reverses time."

It was around this time that Dad's doctor told him his cancer was officially in remission. Five years had passed with no recurrences. We didn't celebrate when we got the news because we *knew*. We had always known. That evening, I picked up the phone when my brother called and told him. "Yo, how fucked would it have been if Pops died of cancer when you were in jail? That would have been so fucked, bro. But I knew."

"Yeah. Would have been fucked," he answered.

The operator interrupted: "One more minute until this phone call ends."

Tiny cleared his throat. "But I knew, too, bro. I knew."

I was inching closer to thirty but it didn't feel like that. I'd started sleeping over at the apartment I'd lived in with my ex-girlfriend again; started leaving a few pairs of boxers and socks and jeans over there. At home, Pops fell asleep while watching the eleven o'clock news every night, and Mom yelled at him every morning when she found new cigarette burns on the couch's throw pillows. I went to work, then went to the gym, then came home, then complained about the meat being overcooked. I lived for the weekend, got drunk on Friday nights, rehydrated and cheered for Ohio State on Saturdays, and watched NFL football on Sundays. Time passed, but nothing changed.

And then I came home one evening and everything did.

Mom went to a walk-in clinic after the uneasy feeling in her stomach wouldn't go away. When the probiotics she was told to take didn't work, she went back. They gave her a prescription and told her that if the pills didn't work to see a family doctor. She was fond of doctors but not doctor appointments. Mom liked to work on her own schedule and the walk-in clinic was sufficient; it was a twenty-minute walk from our home so she didn't have to wait on my dad for a ride over. Mom never balked at a twenty-minute walk. She was so strong. And she never tired.

But when the pills didn't work, she figured that a trip to the doctor was worth the hassle.

"So what did the doctor say?" I asked when I got home one day in mid-November.

"Ah, I have to go back and do some tests. More bullshit. These doctors can never just give you a straight answer," Mom replied. "He told me to eat more red meat. One day red meat is bad for you; the next day it's good. Always some bullshit with these doctors, you know."

I was already on my way downstairs. "Yup," I called back up at her. "That's why I always used to ask for McDonald's on Friday nights. Same difference at the end of the day."

"Burgers from the grocery store are way cheaper. Just wait until you have your own place and have to pay your own bills one day, Parkayyy."

I didn't bother responding.

It was only when I noticed that Dad had driven Mom to the grocery store that I realized she must have gotten the results from the new doctor's test. I was playing a video game when Pops walked into the house for the second time carrying grocery bags from the car. "Pops, you being a manly man today, eh?" I joked. "Why are you bringing in all these bags? Where's Mom at?"

"She's coming," he said. A minute later she walked up the stairs.

I put my game on pause. "Mom, you alright? Your stomach still bothering you that bad?"

"I'm fine, son. Just tired. I've been tired lately."

For as long as I could remember, Mom only ever appeared tired in the mornings. Her second coffee, we'd learned at a young age, was a good marker for when it was safe to strike up basic conversations. Before that second cup, you risked heavy fire targeting all the things you'd fucked up the previous day. "You fuckers eat cereal at night and can't even close the bag properly? Do you not know where your mouth is when you're eating food downstairs? How 'bout one of you pick up a vacuum for once? All the sports you play and you can't be bothered to cut the grass and instead wait on your dad to do it? Do you not know how to aim your piss into the toilet? I swear it's like I'm living with three blind fools." When she was tired, Mom was all fire and brimstone.

But this was different. After a weekend sleep-in until two in the afternoon or the quick nap after she got home from work, I never saw Mom lacking energy. She would read, watch TV, help with homework, prepare side dishes for dinner, talk to neighbours on the phone, wash dishes after dinner, clean up after washing dishes, talk to neighbours outside, watch more TV, and clean again once after "all you assholes went to bed." (*Assholes* was a term of endearment in my home. I loved her for the way she established the Morris household vernacular. The way we kept inside words in and left the outside world out.) But this tired was different. It made her move and talk slowly.

"So, how did those tests go?" I asked.

"Ah, they booked me in for December. More tests. What do you want for dinner, Matthew?" She was calm, patient, *tired*.

"I don't know. You feel like McDonald's? I can drive over there once I'm done this game," I offered.

"No. We just got groceries. Maybe steak. Some red meat."

I was going to remind her that Big Macs and Quarter Pounders with cheese also had red meat in them but I stopped myself. This new kind of tired gave me pause. The mom I knew and loved had seemingly changed overnight. Time had somehow fast-forwarded and showed me Mom in a way I hadn't seen before.

"December? That's the next time you see the doctor?"

"Yes. Sometime in early December," she answered, after handing Pops steaks to put on the barbecue. I finished my video game. I lost, a bit upset that my momentum dipped after taking a few minutes' break to talk to Mom. Minutes that I was frustrated I could never get back.

———

In early December I didn't have to remind myself that Mom was getting the test results that we all had been secretly waiting for. *Secretly* waiting on because life wasn't normal with Mom so tired and so skinny.

Despite those changes, she was still strong. She still hawked my bagels with cream cheese, complaining that the herb and garlic flavour only went on sale rarely, and the way I was using it, it wouldn't last for more than three bagels. Maybe two, the way I was slathering it on.

"Bagels come in packs of six. You're a teacher, Matthew. Too bad the schools you work at don't teach economics. You would need to sit in a class or two for those lessons." I couldn't help but stare at her and laugh. She was getting older in front of my eyes. Something I noticed but also didn't really notice. *Really* didn't notice.

I came home from work a little later than usual that day. I was tired too. The door slammed behind me, not because I wanted it to, but because I couldn't wait to get inside, out of the cold.

"Sorry. That was a little loud. It's cold as shit soon as five p.m. hits these days." I rubbed my arms. "We need chili or soup tonight for dinner, I swear. It's too damn cold already this winter." I took a deep breath. Another day at work done and another evening back at home. I'd survived the time I had earlier wished away.

Mom was standing at the top of the steps, looking down at me.

I wanted to ask about her test results, and at the same time I wanted her to just tell me. Instead she stood silently at the top of the steps, forcing me to reconcile time with reality, with her. "So?" I started. "What did the doctor say?"

Sometimes eyes can speak words; sometimes eyes can tell time. I stood there looking at my beautiful, tired, strong, soft, solid, shrinking mom. And she looked back at me.

"So . . . ? What the fuck, Mom. You're making me nervous just staring at me. What did they say?" The last four words came out of my mouth slowly. Hesitantly.

Her pause awakened dark and heavy fears inside my chest.

"How was your day, son?" Her words seemed to float above her like clouds. She asked again, "So, how was your day?"

"Mom. Are you serious? Stop the nonsense. What did the doctor say?"

She looked at me, right into my eyes. "I have cancer."

Time stopped.

"Okay . . . okay. That's alright. Fucking cancer, eh. Pops had it. He's good. We'll be fine."

She relaxed, almost as if she was taking her first deep breath in minutes. "Yeah, cancer." Her voice was stronger, more affirmed, less tired. She took another long pause, then walked into the kitchen. "We'll be fine."

We ate ice cream that night. The only thing I remember asking her was what type of cancer they told her she had. "Pancreatic," she responded. "Apparently that's why the clinic thought it was a stomach flu or something. Fucking clinic doctors. Quacks."

"I'll buy some Gatorade tomorrow," I responded. "Stupid doctors and bullshit cancer, as if we don't have enough to deal with." I'd never heard of that type of cancer and told myself not to research it on the Internet. Google would take me down a rabbit hole where worst-case scenarios popped up first. For the first time in weeks, I thought about my brother. Jealous that he was away and not having to bear the thousand-pound grey cloud I felt on my chest. "We'll be fine. Are you feeling fine? We'll be alright," I said. I was answering my own questions, reassuring myself. I was accustomed to living in the silence that time affords.

"I'm fine, Matthew. Don't worry. I'm just tired."

For the first time, I was struck as being *tired* too. "Yeah, I hear you, Mom," I said. I was listening. Finally listening. Almost wishing I hadn't come home that evening. Wishing I could either rewind or fast-forward. Anything that would get me to a better moment.

On Christmas Eve, my parents and I got into my car and drove to Aunt Ena's for our traditional family get-together. My aunt's house, filled with my cousins and the usual love that accompanies gift-giving and gravy on top of steaming mashed potatoes, felt a touch colder to me that night. I sipped on sorrel, playing card games with my cousins, while Mom, Shelly, and my aunt sat on the couch talking to each other in whispers. I watched the younger ones rip through the few presents they were allowed to open and run around the house with their new toys, begging their older relatives to play with them. I thought back to when I was around ten, how oblivious I was to the world around me. When I didn't have to think about being Black or being grown. When I had everything I needed without even realizing it.

I hoped that the two-week winter break from teaching would recharge me before I headed into the new year. I was exhausted. Sleep was becoming a task. My mind wandered to a thousand places at once. For some reason, Mom getting cancer wasn't like Dad getting cancer; I didn't feel the same way. Maybe it was her eyes, or the weight she had lost when she was dieting, or the food she left untouched, or her walks that got shorter and shorter. Her cancer was different from my dad's.

I pulled up to a friend's house in early January, a few days before we both had to go back to work. "You've been out of it lately, Matthew. Something is off with you. I can tell," she said as we sat on her front porch.

I lit a cigarette that I had taken from home. I didn't even smoke. For some reason, a cigarette felt appropriate. "My mom," I said, coughing a phlegmy silver cloud out into the air. "She was diagnosed with cancer."

She looked up, surprised. "I'm sorry. My uncle just finished his last round of chemo. Cancer, you know, that disease touches so many families. It's messed up."

I knew what she was trying to do. I had told myself the same thing a hundred times in the last few weeks. Finding a common enemy was a method I had used to feel better about myself, my circumstances, and the way others looked at my Blackness, for years. This time, that common enemy was not attacking me but my mom. Attacking the person who had guided me. Attacking the only white person in my life I unquestioningly loved. I closed my eyes and felt the nighttime breeze on my face. Then I put the cigarette to my lips and took another draw.

"What type of cancer does she have?" she asked.

"Um. Pancreatic," I said, opening my eyes to look at her.

Her eyes widened as she gasped. "Uhhh, that's one of the worst ones."

I knew she didn't mean to say it like that, but I couldn't help but grow angry. I looked at her and said, "Thanks. Good to know." I butted out the cigarette on her steps and got up to walk inside.

"I'm sorry, Matthew," she said.

I was sorry too. At that moment, I was sorry that prior to that night, I hadn't used the word *sorry* enough. Sorry that I hadn't ever really thought about being sorry.

By the start of second semester, I was a shell of myself. Mom was too. She cleaned less and less and slept more and more. Into the evening, she would call for me to come upstairs. I would pause my video game or take a break from working on a lesson plan.

"I've reminded you a couple times already this week, Matthew. Can you please not shove the bread to the back of the fridge when you're done with it?" Toast was something she still ate on a regular basis. Always with her coffee. She didn't explain why putting the bread back in the fridge was no longer good enough, but she didn't yell at me for the bread being out of reach either. She asked me with a new patience and affability I hadn't experienced from her before.

"Yeah, no problem, Mom. My bad," I would answer. "Is that it?" When she nodded her head, I'd say, "Okay. Love you," before heading back downstairs. Mom never held back on using those two words with me—whether she was tucking me into bed as a child or wishing me a safe trip back to college as a man. "Love you too," she'd respond. Despite how much we'd changed over the years, that part did not.

A few doses of radiation therapy did nothing to shrink the tumour. When Mom told me that we were going to try chemotherapy, I shrugged my shoulders and asked when the first round was. "Are you scared?" I asked.

"No. They say I'm going to feel like shit after for a few days and my hair will fall out, but fuck it, I've been wanting to cut my hair for a while."

I loved how she used profanity. Even as a little kid I was enamoured of it. At ten, when my babysitter complained to Mom that I was swearing around other kids, she told me that I should be careful how I speak around people because they would judge me by the words I used. She didn't chastise me for using the words themselves. And she didn't tell me that because I would grow up to become a Black man, I should be more careful with my language, tone, and disposition around other people, especially white babysitters. She didn't lecture me on the double standard I would have to endure for a lifetime because she decided to marry a Black man and have me. She just told me to be careful. And to say sorry the next time.

"Yeah." I laughed. "We'll go out to one of the beauty salons around Markham and Lawrence and get you a nice wig."

"I'm thinking something in between Jackie O and Beyoncé," she said, smiling.

I laughed. "You can wear the Jac-Oncé style for a few months. Until your hair grows back."

"Yup. When my hair grows back, then the pressure will be on. I think my hair will look better than both of them. Don't you think?"

"Absolutely, Mom." I was not lying. Mom, in the last few months, had become the most beautiful woman I had ever seen.

My students were getting on my nerves, and my girlfriend had become my ex again. The cold, dark, damp winter days of February in Canada were wearing me down as usual. I was looking forward to March Break and a trip out of town with my boys, already planned and booked. We spent nights watching Raptors games, talking about what clubs we planned to go to, what numbers we planned to bet on in the casino, and what alcohol we'd buy once we arrived. I was over winter and its drudgery. I told my brother I would take some pictures for him and keep my phone on roam at all times in case he wanted to three-way call one of his friends while I was out of town. I wasn't going too far. Only a ninety-minute drive to Niagara Falls.

I had reverted back into full-grown adult mode—counting away weekdays, waiting for weekends, and letting my imagination run wild with thoughts about the future. Home, once again, became a one-stop shop for nourishment and sleep. Things like time, safety, and love were there but pushed to the background. Instead of acting thirty years old, I morphed back into acting twenty. When everything revolved around me. When my survival outweighed everything else.

I noticed the porch light was on earlier than usual as I parked my car in the driveway. I kicked the snow off my boots before coming inside. Mom was always a stickler for that. "Home a little late. What did y'all make for dinner?" I asked before climbing the steps up to the living room. "Mom, please don't tell me you made scalloped potatoes again. I swear I'm developing an allergy."

No one answered me.

"Why the hell aren't any lights on? Hello, it's only eight o'clock." Still no answer. At the top of the stairs I noticed the TV was off.

"Is the power out or something? Pops, why are you just sitting there without the TV on? Aren't the Leafs playing tonight or something?" I popped my head into the kitchen. Empty.

"Pops?"

Dad cleared his throat. "Your mom is in the hospital."

I walked toward him, stared, and stopped. "Quit fucking around," I said. I didn't even wait for a response. I walked to my parents' bedroom, the room only my dad used now. The TV was off and she wasn't in there. I checked the room she'd slept in for the last five years—my childhood room—its walls inscribed with inspirational quotes that I'd written in Sharpie, making her furious. The bed was immaculately made, and she wasn't there.

"Pops, quit playing. I can't believe you got Mom to go along with this bullshit. It's late, man," I said to him as I checked my brother's bedroom. The room that no one slept in. The room that was reserved for him once he came home from prison. "Mom?"

Empty.

I hopped downstairs. Maybe she was doing laundry and Pops had caught me coming home at the perfect time. That guy, my dad, always playing stupid little jokes. I ran to the laundry room, turned on the lights, and looked around.

Nothing.

The main room in the basement. Nothing.

I wondered if she was in my room. Maybe she'd finished the laundry and was putting away some of my clothes. I'd told her repeatedly that I could do my own laundry and put away my own things but she still did it. I told her that coming home and seeing my boxers folded up on my bedspread was weird, but she laughed and told me that I'd probably mess up the washing machine and piss her off even more if I did it myself. Even in her sixties, she was holding onto mothering me. I secretly loved that. I flipped the lights before I walked in. "Mom?"

She wasn't there either.

Pops never ever lied to me. Pops never ever said sorry either. He didn't have to.

Back upstairs I stared at my dad. Waited for him to say something more.

"She's in the hospital, son."

I collapsed onto the couch beside him. The back of my head almost hit the wall as my body crumbled deep into the cushion. It was an old couch that we had said we'd replace five years ago but never got around to. "Why?" I asked. I wasn't looking for a response and he knew it. "Why?" I asked again.

The hospital greeted me with an unfamiliar odour, a wafting smell of industrial sanitizer and dried urine. Pops and I peeked into room after room on the eighth floor. The nurse at the patient information centre had told us the room number, but by the time we got off the elevator we had both forgotten it. Her words—"the cancer care floor"—kept reverberating inside my head. I wrestled with what *cancer* and *care* might look like in a hospital. And if the most prestigious hospitals in the city smelled the same as Scarborough General.

"There she is. How are you doing today, my lady?" Pops smiled at the sight of Mom, after taking a few steps into the sixth room we checked. "Feeling better?"

I didn't recognize Pops' voice. It was much slower than usual. Gentler. As if his words were holding onto a secret that only he knew.

"I'm fine, Neville. How are you?" She spoke in a similarly clement manner. For those few brief seconds, I froze, hearing them speak to each other in a way that I'd forgotten. A way that came only after decades spent together in shared dependency. I studied Mom. It had only been a little over a day since I last saw her, but she looked different. The hospital gown revealed so much of what I hadn't noticed in the previous months. How clearly the vertebrae of her spine knuckled out. How the skin under her arms sagged. Before she spoke to me, for a brief moment, I forgot I existed.

"Hi, Matthew," she exclaimed with a bright smile. "So, I guess you heard the news, eh?"

"Yeah. I did—um, no. No, not really. What news? I came home last night and Pops told me you were here. For the longest time, I actually thought he was joking. Why the hell are you in the hospital, Mom?" I cleared my throat. "What did they say? When are you coming home?"

"Just a precaution, Matthew," she answered. "It's quicker here, I guess." She was sharing a room with three other people. An older man wearing an oxygen mask was staring at flashing pictures from a thirteen-inch television that jutted out from the wall. An elderly lady was whispering with a woman I assumed was her daughter. Someone else was sleeping in the bed ten feet across from Mom.

"Let's close the drapes a bit," I said, sliding the thin grey curtain in front of the elderly woman and her daughter. "You should have some privacy if you're going to be here for a day or two."

"A few days, they said," Mom responded. "And believe me, I got better rest here last night than at home listening to your dad snoring his brains out while I worried he would burn down the house with a cigarette in his mouth." Dad laughed until he didn't. I chuckled, but I knew she was lying. She was still trying to protect me.

We talked until a nurse came to tell us that visitation hours were over.

"Make sure you two keep the house clean. If it's a pigsty when I get home, both of you will have hell to pay."

I laughed until I didn't and then gave her a goodbye kiss on her cheek. "Alright, Mom. Don't worry about home. I'll hold it down until you get back."

"Okay. Love you."

"Love you too."

Our house felt empty without Mom there. When I'd left home at nineteen, I didn't consider how my parents might have felt not having their oldest son under their gaze. I figured that it was the natural evolution endured by all families. Parents raising their children, gradually giving them responsibilities so that they'd be able to navigate their own lives, their own worlds, independently.

I didn't want to live with my parents forever and could safely assume, through their words, that they didn't want that either. Mom and Dad had been working their entire lives to nurture my development—to help me grow into a man who could navigate the world on his own. I was lucky to grow up under them. Mom especially had tried her best to instill in me the right amount of love, freedom, and wisdom to ensure that I survived. She had used her white skin to blanket my Black body from the destruction that the outside world—the things beyond her control—forced upon me. It took me thirty years to see what she had known all along.

I didn't ask too many questions when she told me she had to stay at the hospital for a few more days. Mom asked me if I thought her lifelong addiction to cigarettes was the cause of her cancer. By the time she asked me, I had done some research. Google told me things I didn't want to know. So I lied to her.

Shelly, Aunt Ena, Uncle Bernie, his wife, and their sons all made regular visits to Mom while Dad and I sat bedside. Tiny would try to time his calls for the evening, when he knew we would be there, so he could talk to Mom. When the room was quiet enough, I would put my phone on speaker so that I could listen to them. Every night, when they talked, I sat in a chair near the foot of the hospital bed, struck by how my mom and brother were both in arresting situations neither of them had anticipated. My brother tended to dwell on the people he'd thought were friends who gave evidence against him in court. Mom spoke mostly about the future.

Those phone calls my brother made from prison eventually turned into family chats. With Dad and I seated in chairs beside mom's hospital bed and Tiny on the phone, the drapes closed around us, we talked about TV shows and who would shovel the driveway tomorrow, the lessons I taught in class earlier that day that hadn't gone as planned. Every day, the four of us convened and shared parts of our stories to pass the time. The same time that all four of us were trying to fight off. To get back. And at the end of every night, before we all had to go our separate ways, we all said the same three words to each other. *Love you too.*

When all four of us talked together, no one lied.

Mom was careful with her words while she was in the hospital. This was normal; she was always careful outside home. I had learned that lesson from her after the debacle with the white babysitter. I had learned to present only the parts of myself, when outside, that protected my insides. Inside the sanctuary of our family, we learned to dote accordingly. When Mom told Tiny, "I'd like to see you before I go globetrotting," I knew that she was holding onto a secret. And when I heard her say that, my insides knotted themselves so tightly that I didn't know how to release them.

She said it so casually that it took me a few minutes to understand. Mom tended to use blunt phrases and casual exaggerations, and we'd learned not to take it literally or personally. We knew we weren't going to "fuck the whole entire fridge up," if we stared into it for longer than six seconds, the same way we knew we weren't going to cost Mom "a thousand fucking dollars" if we held the front door open on hot summer days. She'd spent years curating a space we could call home. The warnings we received when we let inside things out—from gaped fridges to open screen doors—were simply tests, microcosms, of how we ought to look at the bigger world. Home base was a resting stop but also a final point. My aunt Mavis knew what Mom was now learning—*home* is both entry and departure. A poetry of opposites. And going away and coming back home are not mutually exclusive but instead necessary for growth. For life.

But this new hyperbole, uttered in a bed she didn't and couldn't make week after week, hit me differently. Unlike most of her exaggerations, this one had truth behind it. Truth that I didn't want to wrestle with.

Her body continued to shrink before my eyes. Her skin loosened around her bones. Her eyes became the wettest ones I'd ever seen. "Can you bring me that old laptop that you don't use anymore?" she asked.

"The Toshiba one? Yeah, no problem."

"Yeah. That one. The old thick grey one. Can I borrow it? Because I'd like to continue watching my shows while I'm here. Put a bunch of episodes from *Law & Order*, *Grey's Anatomy*, and *Breaking Bad* on there. Put only the newest ones. From the last few weeks. And maybe a few movies too."

"What movies?" I asked.

"Good ones. You know the ones I like. Realistic movies. Something to keep me watching."

I spent the evening uploading Mom's favourite shows onto a USB and double-checked to make sure they worked on the computer.

"Okay. First off, you have to keep this computer plugged in. If you unplug it, it will die." I said the next day. "If you're watching your shows and the nurse comes in, don't let her unplug the power cord. Or else I'm going to have to come back and show you how to restart the whole thing. Which is a pain in the ass because it takes so long."

I still did not know how words and ideas that seem so opposite are actually in sync.

I knew I was tired. More tired than I had ever been at any point in my life. Pops too. I could see on his face that the nightly trips to the hospital wore away at him. He drank more and more alcohol to keep going. I did too.

I was ordering a Baconator combo from Wendy's on my lunch break when Uncle Bernie called. My uncle never called me. "Matthew. How are you doing? Are the kids at school giving you a hard time yet?"

I laughed into the phone as the drive-through worker handed me my Sprite. "Not yet," I said.

"Listen, Matthew. The chemo has not worked. The doctors told your mom the cancer is in stage four. They are transferring her to the palliative care unit."

I hadn't heard the words *palliative care* before and I didn't know how many stages cancer had. "Okay. Um, so what floor is that on?" I asked. I wanted to get back to school so that I could eat slowly and use the bathroom before afternoon classes.

"It's on the sixth floor, Matthew." He paused. "Your mother is not coming home. We need to start making arrangements."

I didn't have a response for him. He wasn't a doctor; what did he know? For that matter, what did they know? They were the reason why she was in the hospital in the first place. And I needed to get back to work. I wanted to eat my fries while they were still hot.

"Okay . . . Alright. That's a lot to process. Arrangements . . . I get it." I was lying. We said our goodbyes and I got back to school in time to sit in the staff room and dip my hot fries in ketchup.

Mom's room on the sixth floor seemed bigger and a bit brighter than the last. There were only two beds in it. She had a window facing west, looking down Lawrence Avenue. We used to ride the bus together on Lawrence to go Christmas shopping at Scarborough Town Centre. Beside the window was a whiteboard screwed into the wall. I read the remnants of erased writings on it: *we love you*. I wondered what those other families looked like who had gathered here not so long ago, who used the same words we used.

Love, I thought, leaves indelible marks on us all.

The trip my boys and I planned for Niagara Falls finally arrived. In the last few months, I had started telling my boys that I loved them. They told me they loved me. Despite that, there were only a few times our conversations moved outside games, girls, and materialistic goals. Sharing our dreams and fears was still uncomfortable. Kevin's mom had passed away a decade before I met him in university, and none of us ever talked about it. On the phone the night before our trip, I told him, "I really need to break bread with you. I have so many questions, bro."

"I know," he said.

At the gas station before we got on Highway 401, Shelly called. "Cuz, are you sure about going to Niagara Falls this weekend? You know, the doctors said she has—"

"I know what they said, cousin. I know. Mom ain't dying though," I told her. I didn't want to hear more about what other people said or thought about Mom. "My mom isn't dying. Not this weekend. I know it. C'mon. Trust me. I know." I was still willing my words in Mom's direction. Something I'd been doing since I was a child.

"Okay, cuz. I get it. We'll be by and pick up Pops to visit her. I get it, cuz. I love you." She paused. "We'll hold it down while you're gone. Go do what you need to do. I get it."

"Thank you," I told her. "I love you."

When I next visited her in the hospital, Mom's eyes were wetter and heavier than I'd ever seen them. That scared me. On some nights it would take her minutes to respond to my questions. That scared me. I still had so many questions that I needed her to answer. On other nights, Dad and I would sit quietly in her room, me scrolling through my phone, him at the foot of her bed with the same heavy stare at her silky face, her damp hair, her ropy hands, her sharp knee caps under her light blankets. Back and forth and over again. Waiting for her to wake up. Hoping that this night spent in her presence wouldn't be our last. Some nights she woke up, but other times we spent our whole visit watching her sleep.

Thinking about that scared me. Time started to scare me.

The first Sunday in March was the eleventh straight Sunday that me, Pops, and Mom spent hours together at Scarborough General Hospital. I'd gotten used to the smell, the stupid visitor parking prices, and the stale bagels from the Tim Hortons in the main lobby.

We'd arrived early because visiting hours on Sunday ended earlier than on weeknights. It was warm for early March, so when

I settled into my usual chair, I took off my jacket and shoes. This place, over time, had become home too.

Mom lay in the bed quietly, opening her eyes when she heard us walk in. Eyes smiling a tired-looking smile. Eyes that were so wet. Pops was talking to himself, talking to her, talking about the dishes he'd washed earlier and the food he'd cooked before coming and the game he was planning to watch later on. When he started talking about old times, I shoved my phone into the pocket of my jacket and listened to him. He talked about the time she'd tried acid at a friend's house thirty-five years earlier, then about the apartment they'd rented at Yonge and Avenue. He reminded her of the time the elevator was out of service and she refused his demands that he carry all the bags up the four flights of stairs even though she was pregnant. With me. He talked about the first house they bought in Malvern twenty-five years ago and the time she practised driving in an empty parking lot and almost had a panic attack. That was twenty years ago, he said.

I had heard Mom and Dad laugh about all of those times before. But I had never really listened. This time I did.

"Matthew, did we tell you that the same doctor who is helping Mom now is the same doctor that gave birth to you? Well, not gave birth to you, but the doctor—Doctor Sorensam, Doctor Sumnersall—you know the doctor's name. Her cancer doctor now, when you were born, he was our doctor for you." Pops stumbled as he redirected the conversation he was having with Mom to me.

"Yeah, you both told me when Mom first came here. Crazy, eh," I said, "how the world works." I knew about the doctor, but it was a distraction from what was staring us in the face.

"Small world, eh, son," Pops said with his eyes closed and head down. I stared at him and then at Mom. Her eyes were open but everything else about her was closing. I could feel it. That scared me more.

It had been so long since I had depended on Mom's strength, but the last eleven weeks had depleted my ability to exist without her. I got off my chair and crawled beside Mom in her bed. I needed to be beside her. Beside the woman who had taught me so much, given me so many things, and nurtured my growth with her guidance. I thought about all the times she protected my insides. And all the times she guided my outsides. I thought about how her body, even in its frail state, was still the strongest body I knew. And how I still had so much to learn about being a Black man from the coldest, realest, most mushy-hard, loving white woman to ever exist.

"Mom." My lips touched her ear as I whispered. For the last couple hours, she hadn't said anything. "Mom," I repeated. This time her wet eyes opened wide and lit up. I watched her mouth, waiting for her words. Her lips had begun to curl inwards. It was something I hadn't noticed until I had gotten right beside her in bed.

"Mom. I know that everything you did for me was meant to shape me so that I could survive and be happy with myself. I've been happy for so long. As long as I can remember, thanks to you, Mom. Thank you, Mom. You did an amazing job. You were—are the best mother I could have ever asked for, Mom. I have so many other things to say. And other things to tell you. But time is messed up, Mom. And I'm tired. And I know you're tired, too, Mom. I can tell. Mom, you know you did everything right for me, Mom." I stopped talking so that I wouldn't choke. "Mom, I can't believe this. But I have to." My eyes grew as wet as hers. "It's okay, Mom," I said in between deep shuddering breaths. "It's okay."

Mom looked out the window the whole time, but I knew she was hearing me. The same way I had heard her all those times when she told me things I wanted to hear but acted like I didn't. "It's okay, Mom," I whispered into her ear. "It's okay. You can let go. I love you. We love you. We'll be alright. You can let go."

Mom's eyes never left the window that faced west, looking down on Lawrence Avenue East. I kissed her for hundreds of seconds on her earlobe, her cheek, her forehead, her caving mouth, her chin, her hands. Her strong hands that had held and guided me for as long as I could remember. For as long as I could remember, for all of time.

"Mom. Come home."

"Hi, it's half past six." A nurse had popped her head in the doorway. "We let you stay an extra thirty minutes, but visiting hours on Sunday are over at six p.m."

"Okay, Nurse," Dad said after looking up at the clock.

We stayed another thirty minutes with Mom.

Talking to ourselves, talking to her. Leaving that night, I'd never felt so full and empty at the same time. So knowing about what time would bring next. So boyish and mannish in the same breath. So understanding of what *support, context, patience, happiness, sadness, loneliness, independence, validation,* and *character* meant. So aware of how time and love travel outside our bodies and outside our breath. I'd never felt so depleted inside but complete on the outside. Complete with the knowledge that right and wrong are deeper than our skin.

I'd never felt so much my mother's son. So at home.

A PIECE OF MY BLACK CHARACTER

At thirty-four years old, I had wounds in my life that I alone created. They festered and swelled and made me feel like the only way I could handle them was to get drunk with my boys and laugh at our mistakes. Every time I got another tattoo or earring or new clothing felt like an out-of-body experience. Later on, each drink anchored me back to where I'd started. Each silent second I had alone with my thoughts added up, piled on, and eventually made me. What I was left with was the person I needed to become. I think I became who I am in part because it was what I innately gravitated toward, and in part because I learned my character so well that it eventually felt natural to become it.

On a Wednesday night, I was drunk and joking around with one of my childhood friends, Gio. My brother, three years after being released from prison, was working a night shift at the Magna factory in Woodbridge. I was happy that he wasn't still inside a prison or outside *on road*, but instead working, making an hourly wage. My dad, a few years removed from helplessly trying to move on after my mother died, was drunk too, half a bottle of Rémy in. My boy, Gio—one of only two or three white men I've ever vested trust in—was eight Heinekens down and rambling about how much better Conor McGregor was than any Black UFC fighter who'd ever entered the Octagon.

Despite Gio's physical inability to stand up without wavering, his argument was strong. That didn't annoy me. His ease at deflecting the aspect of race did. So, instead of using words to express my frustration, I pushed him. He pushed me back. I grabbed him, wanting to show that at any moment, at any time, that white rationale, however coherent and clever it comes off, doesn't mean shit to Black abundance when Black people know they're right. A thing outside me and inside me propelled me into him.

He tried to overpower me, but I gripped the shoulders of his T-shirt to prevent any counter. I twisted his body off the floor and spun him sideways through the air. I was too drunk to notice that mere seconds earlier my dad had crept up behind Gio to join in on the banter. As I twisted my bestest white-boy friend off the ground, his body collided with my aging father. Pops' body flew into the air and then landed. He lay still on the floor near the dining room lamp. The same lamp that had been there long before I got my first tattoo, long before I got my first earring, long before I learned who Snoop Doggy Dogg was.

Gio and I stopped jostling and laughed about our tussle. My dad groaned. "C'mon, Pops," we both told him numerous times. He didn't get up and barely moved. "Stop acting like a bitch," I said. He stopped groaning and just lay there. At thirty-four years old, on a Wednesday night, I had no idea that I had just broken my own dad.

I went to the kitchen to get ice. I walked back to the living room to put the ice in my cup. I poured another drink. "Pops, for real. You're one helluva actor. I think you missed your life's calling—Denzel," I said.

Dad didn't respond. He just lay there with his face on the wood flooring.

"I think he may be hurt, man. Pops, are you hurt for real? The joke is over, man," Gio asked. Pops wouldn't respond. Gio shifted his gaze from my dad to me. "I think he's really hurt, man."

I rolled my eyes and walked over to my lying father. "C'mon. Get up. Here we go," I said as I bent down to scoop him up and carry him to the couch. It had been about fifteen years since my dad's presence intimidated me. When I was a child, he was the man I looked up to. The man I could always count on to be at my football games cheering from the stands, yelling, "Let's gooo, Matthew!" I was so happy that he was proud of me when my high school team won the city championship. At home, hours after the game, I watched him beam as he watched the local news show our team highlights and an interview with me.

When I would return home on break from college, one of the first things we would always do was flex side by side and have Mom judge whose biceps were bigger. At sixteen, I took in every tip he gave me as he sat in the passenger seat of his car and explained that I needed to drive with two hands on the wheel and check both my rear-view mirror and my blind spot before changing lanes.

On this Wednesday night, the ease with which I was able to pick up his scrawny body sobered me. He had always been a tightly packed man with no room on his frame for fat or a belly despite the copious amounts of beer and liquor he consumed. But a shot ran through my brain as I lowered him onto the couch. My hero couldn't have weighed more than 120 pounds now. And I had seen this story before.

As Dad lay on the couch in silence, Gio and I rambled on about the authenticity of Valentine's Day, the Raptors chances at going for back-to-back championships, and that time in high school when that one kid did that one thing that was dumb as fuck but smart now that we thought about it.

Around midnight, Gio said, "Shit, it's getting late. Maybe we should help the old fella to bed. You want us to help you get into bed, Pops?"

My dad nodded in agreement. Silently. No joke, no comeback, just nodded. I looked at him and then at Gio, who was looking at me. This was unusual. Dad always had a slick line or an "I got ya" after playing the sheep on drunken occasions.

"I'm telling you, you shoulda been an actor," I said as we carried him to his bedroom and lifted him onto the right side of the bed. The same side he'd been sleeping on, alone, for years.

"You need anything, Pops?" I asked humbly. "Water. A lighter. You got your smokes?" It sunk in that he was not playing around with us for some final one-up joke.

"No. They're on the coffee table. Bring my cigarettes and my lighter, son." Thinking about it now, it was one of the first times he'd ever referred to me as *son*. Shit, I thought to myself. Shit.

"Yo, what the fuck did you two drunk assholes do to Pops last night?" my brother said to me the next afternoon. "Fucking guy can't even walk properly. I had to help him onto the toilet."

I stared at Tiny with a look mixed between disgust and questioning. "Get the fuck outta here," I punched back. "This guy snuck up behind me and Gio when we were wrestling around and fell down. Barely fell hard. What the hell you talking about, helping him to the toilet . . . Shit." The last word spilled out of my consciousness but was said patronizingly enough that it sounded like I was complaining about Pops' long period of grieving. "Always looking for someone to feel sympathy for him." Selfishness and trauma and hurt and pain, which I'd been grappling with for the last five years, came through my words.

"Whatever. You're a fucking asshole, and you and Gio need to grow the fuck up. Getting so drunk that you start fighting each other. And all the time too. One of you idiots is gonna end up in the hospital one day. You know what would happen to you two clowns if you acted like that in prison?"

I walked into the kitchen, pissed off and frustrated. "Don't care what would happen 'cause I ain't never going to jail, yo. He's fine, yo. Pops is fine."

"Stupid, bro. Pour me a drink," Tiny said from a room away.

On Friday afternoon I came home to find Dad lying on the couch. The same couch I'd put him on Wednesday night and in the same position that Tiny said he had stayed in all Thursday.

"Are you really that hurt, Pops?" I asked him.

He looked at me, then looked back at the television.

"Because if you are, we should probably go to the hospital."

He looked back over to me and shrugged his shoulders without saying anything. His jaw was closed as he shrugged, and I remembered that the $4,000 dentures that his sister Ena, Tiny, and I had persuaded him to get had been sitting on the bathroom counter instead of inside his mouth for weeks. Despite the years that had passed, the thought of entering a hospital still gave us all pause.

"Alright. We're going. Might as well get you checked out by some doctors anyways. It's been awhile. Thirty minutes," I said.

"No Scarborough General," he said.

"Of course not," I said, thinking how those three words were the first three words he had said to me in two days. "Thirty minutes. Then we're rolling," I repeated.

Some nurses helped my father undress and slip into a blue hospital robe before gurneying him off for an MRI. I watched as they loaded him onto the examination bed and gave him instructions to be still while inside the machine. The bones of his spine met his skin in a way that I didn't expect. *Shit.* 120 pounds, maybe. Maybe 110.

"Pops, you good?" I asked sheepishly.

"Yeah, I'm fine, son," he replied. *Son . . . Son . . . Son . . .* That word from my father. Had he ever said that word to me before Wednesday?

"So his hemoglobin is low," the resident doctor told us back in the emergency ward. "Thank God you brought him in. Another day may have been drastic. Neville, we're going to take your weight and run a couple more blood tests. It looks like you have a stress fracture in your hip, something that can heal on its own over time. You should be back at home and sleeping in your own bed tonight, once we're through with a few small things here. Okay?"

Dad nodded and smiled at the doctor. "Thank you, sir. Sorry to bother you but, you know, these things sometimes happen. They call me Pops these days. I'm an old guy now," he added with a laugh. Dad always had a way of making everyone else, especially people in positions of power and especially white men, feel more special than him. "I'm hoping to catch the end of the third period. You know the Leafs. Always good before the leaves fall off the trees. Never good after that," he said with a bright smile and another chuckle. This Jamaican man could talk hockey with anyone. I wondered if he'd become who he was because it was what he innately gravitated toward. Or if he'd learned his character so well that it eventually felt natural to become it too.

Twenty minutes later, a different doctor came in. He seemed weathered by the night shifts he'd spent in hospitals in the east end of the city instead of in the big money, elaborately furnished hospitals downtown on University Avenue. "So, Neville. Your X-rays show bad news. Broken hip. We're going to have to operate."

My heart sunk.

"What does that look like, doctor?" I asked. "Can we make an appointment for his surgery now?"

"You're his son?" He glanced in my direction while shooting off directives to the two nurses beside him.

"Yeah . . . Yes." I replied. "Matthew Morris. *M-O-R-*"

He cut me off. "Yeah, he has a broken hip. Best scenario is full-on hip replacement surgery, given his age and weight." I'd seen a lot of different looks from my dad but I had never seen him look scared.

"Um, oh, oh. Okay. So his hip is broken? Broken. I mean he just fell on the—"

"Yeah, he has a broken hip. Plus his hemoglobin, that's the level of red blood cells . . . We need to operate. He'll stay tonight. I have time tomorrow at four p.m. We'll replace the hip. Some in-patient rehab for a day or so and then physical therapy for a few months post-op. I heard you like the Leafs, Neville. It's 5–2 right now. Tough loss, but hopefully they'll turn it on for the playoffs."

Dad produced a smile and said, "They haven't been good since Wendel Clark. You remember Wendel Clark?" He paused. "I could come back tomorrow; my son Matthew can drive me." He looked at me.

Shit. I had only been this sad one other time in my life. At thirty-four years old, on a Friday night, I realized that my dad had been breaking—for years—in a way that surgery could not fix.

Pops was changed when he came home from the hospital after his operation. So was I. But we both had been for so long already. We had been fighting against something for so many years that it was hard to remember exactly what we were fighting. We waited for time to scab over the wounds we'd endured. A few days was all it took to realize how emotional fractures are tethered to physical snapping points. We were forced to bend so much when we were already so broken.

———

When my brother got out of prison and was allowed to live in a halfway house in Toronto, we visited him with a full cartridge of energy. Time and love and a blood bond was something we understood now. Pain too. Time and love and blood pasteurized our pain. We didn't talk about those things. Instead we talked about Subway sandwiches. I tapped my debit card to pay $32.08 for three subs, a bag of Hickory Sticks, and a fountain pop. I thought about my mom. She would have said I spent too much.

Watching my brother eat, freely, freed me. Watching my dad eat helped me. All three of us had holes inside us that would take time to move beyond. But I was okay with where we were. Safe at that table, inside that Subway, in a city I'd learned to understand, in a country that told me my perceptions were more lies than truth. My father guided me, my mother taught me, and my brother showed me. Every day from then on out seemed different, and yet somehow each new day was never new enough.

After thirty years together as a family, my father, brother, and I survived with our bodies intact. Despite thirty years spent knowing and touching and loving each other, we couldn't be further apart in the routes we had taken to preserve the collective sense of what Black masculinity meant to us. Of what Black boyhood had meant.

After four more months, my brother moved back home. He didn't want to sleep in the room we had preserved for him. The room he had snored in countless nights. The room he used to rush from to get to the TV before me when we were children. He settled into the room where my parents once slept together. Pops took over Daniel's old bedroom. I kept my place downstairs. We were finally back under one roof. Only missing one piece that we would never be able to replace.

Although inevitably we had grown over time into three completely different Black men, we sought for togetherness through tragedy, as many Black men do. The blizzard of unfortunate events that happened to unarmed Black boys and men at the hands of white authority figures barraged my brother's and my Instagram timelines and my dad's nightly newscasts. The senseless deaths of Trayvon Martin, Michael Brown, Freddie Gray, Tamir Rice, and many, many others jolted my understanding of what it meant to be Black. What it meant to come from a father who came by choice to this Indigenous land seeking better opportunities. What it meant to cherish a mother who looked like the people who thought the worst of me. I thought that, now in my thirties, I had survived the worst of folks who looked upon my Black skin rather than my actual character as a person. The rash of disturbing violence against Black boys like me let me know that I'd forever be giving up pieces of myself merely to survive.

Like a lot of Black boys in my position, I thought that the safest thing to do was cover myself with additional layers of white approval.

By the time I entered graduate school at the University of Toronto, I had been teaching in elementary schools for four years and thought I had all the answers. After stepping into a course titled Introduction to Anti-Black Racism Education, all the things I thought I had figured out vanished. PhD candidates spoke endlessly about their research and findings. Words that I had never heard or read in any books whipped through our class dialogue and showed up in fifty-page article after article I was supposed to read in two days. Scholars who hadn't spent a day teaching students chastised the missteps and omissions of the public school system. White folks who claimed authority and ownership of Black experience offered antidotes that promised to reveal, redeem, and revitalize young Black students who were failing their high school courses and "falling through the cracks." Their peers nodded in agreement. I sat there, class after class, struggling to find the right words to say and to write in my papers. Each class was new, but the experience was something I'd felt many times before. Even though I was a grown man, shit always worked out to make me feel like just another Black boy.

When I looked around the classroom in this graduate course, I saw only a sprinkle of Black folk. That was the first reason I muted myself. I didn't know if the lack of Black bodies was a good or bad thing. I couldn't figure out if it was a testament to how hard I'd worked over long, long years. I worried about losing myself in the jargon and academic gymnastics of flipping every Black experience I felt into mere words. Words that everyone also owned. Words that everyone could use equally. Words that diluted *my* experiences as an actual Black man. I'd been scared in my life before. This was a new form of fear.

In those hallways of graduate school, I nodded at the other Black men but we never spoke. Inside those classrooms, they were silent like me. I searched their eyes for connection as certain folks would go on about bodies that looked like ours. I rarely got connecting stares back. It reminded me of late-night subway rides in dark cities. Folks who didn't look like the Black bodies I was looking at talked about why Black bodies that looked like mine "failed in school," were underserved in media and society, and carried burdens of stereotypes and myths unfairly bestowed on them. I looked at these other Black faces. Silence. They talked more about us. We sat there, never making eye contact again. More silence. They gave us their understanding of things we understood deep down in our skin, in our bones, in our guts. I thought I could use the system of white approval to guard against my Black outsides. Each day I found myself imploding.

"What happens inside *our* classrooms is that there is a disconnect within the dichotomy of our Black students and teachers . . ." I closed Facebook on my computer and started to listen more intently.

"The inability to understand the areas our Black youth come from is a major detriment leading to the underservice of particular marked bodies in our communities," they continued.

I was already annoyed. Annoyed that I drove downtown on night after night. Annoyed that it had started to snow again and in two more hours I would have to warm up my car while wiping down my windshield. Annoyed that, for whatever reason, I hadn't owned a pair of winter gloves since I was eight years old, out of my own negligence. Most annoyed that this person claimed to own things about us. About me. Using words flippantly and casually to shove this ownership in my face. *Our* classrooms, *our* communities, *our* Black youth.

If I sat silently, I would be giving another piece of me away. I closed my eyes and hoped, prayed, that they would stop talking. I heard *our* one more time.

"Let me tell you something about what happens to *us*," I said. The words flew out of my mouth before I could think about what to say next. "When a kid who looks like me doesn't do well in class . . ." I paused to look around the room. "That kid is *not* trying in class because he understands how the whole world is looking at him. He's *not* answering questions that the teacher asks because he gets it.

"When a Black kid gets a C minus on a test, he's safe. You know why he's safe? Because if he got an A, he knows the teacher may treat him like he's different. Like he's some type of anomaly simply for getting good grades. What's worse, when he gets that C minus on the test, his friends don't look at him any different. They don't crack jokes about him being 'white-washed' or call him a nerd. He's safe with that C minus. There's less risk. *That's* what happens to *us*."

The room fell silent. I adjusted myself in my chair, scanning the room. A few people were looking back at me, waiting for more. Some had their heads down, jotting notes. The professor broke the silence. "I think Matthew has made some important points. When speaking about Black students, one must come to the realization that we are researching youth. Their actions and articulations of their experiences are not linear with our understanding of how racism operates in schools . . . in the world. They may not know how to name the racism they face. But they indeed experience it. How they express it, how they cope with it, takes on various forms. What Matthew is describing is one integral way that it manifests itself."

I wanted to tell him to shut up, that what I said didn't need to be explained by him.

For the first time, I felt like I was really seen in that academic space. Surrounded by academics, theorists, and scholars who saw the study of anti-Black racism and the Black experience as a career path, I feared that my words may have been taken as an insult to their intelligence. But I needed to be seen and heard, especially as one of the only Black bodies there. Listening to others *other* me over and over was no longer acceptable. It never should have been.

The class session continued for another hour and a half. We dove into analyzing and discussing the remaining readings for the week. Members of the class continually roped their assertions back to my rant. I had nothing else to add to the conversation. I had emptied myself by stepping outside my carefully cultivated character to offer my true self to them. I sat there, wondering how I'd be viewed for the rest of the semester.

"What you said tonight was so on point," Marcus, the only other Black man in the class, said to me after. "I'd been sitting in class for a few weeks now, questioning my own understanding of my experiences as a Black man because everyone around here talks like they've read a million more articles than me." I knew what he really meant. He assumed that I was one of them. Another Black guy who made it to graduate school because he did everything he had been told to do since first grade. The fact that we had never talked outside class amplified his feelings. And I held no grudge against Marcus. Because I had felt the exact same way about him.

I had slipped into seeing other Black men who were successful outside the domains of athletics and entertainment as unlikely anomalies who attained their stature because they were the Carlton Banks type. When Michael Brown was killed and the right wing said that Ferguson police couldn't be racist because the police chief and ninety per cent of the force in that town were Black, I scoffed at the assertion. I knew that capital-R racism didn't work in a black and white manner. And that Black people, too, could operate with racist intentions. It was the reason I changed the way I walked when I passed that police station at four a.m. in Brooklyn. The reason why I was so surprised to see Mahmoud at the University of Toronto before he told me that he was also a student attending classes. And perhaps the same reason why I took playing football and trying to make the NFL so seriously. I knew, regardless of skin colour, we all participated in deeply entrenched racist behaviour in some form or another.

I built pieces of my Black character for parallel reasons. The clothes on my body were judged before I was. My hairstyle, earrings, and tattoos held connotations far deeper than I intended. Marcus and I were the only two Black men in a graduate class titled Introduction to Anti-Black Racism Education, and we didn't even attempt to get to know each other beyond the occasional head nod that said *I see you*.

The remaining weeks of that course did not go as I expected. I was asked to offer my opinions on the other students' thoughts. When I suggested alternative ways to interrogate the literature we were reading, the professor commended my interpretations. As the course went on, I became more of my true self, peeling away layers of the character I'd built. It was becoming clearer that a nerdy, so-called whitewashed version of the true me was acceptable in a way that bucked against the prevailing idea of what it meant to exist as a Black man who ascribed to all parts of Black culture. For the first time, I felt safe as a Black man in a white space.

Only one more thing remained: was I being truly accepted for me or was I a token vessel needed to sharpen up papers and research and ideas? Preparing to enter my thirties, I couldn't escape the feeling of continuously being used. Full safety was always a shade away.

It might always be.

Dad was doing his rehab after coming home from the hospital. Drinking a bit less and eating a bit more. Tiny got his first real job and bought a car using his real name to sign the paperwork, on his own credit. We spent evenings sharing responsibilities and summer afternoons appreciating what we had. All three of us had separately experienced life on both sides. The two sides we experienced—morally right or socially wrong, collective acceptance or social ostracization, life or death—were shaped by the dichotomy everyone experiences. Black or white.

ACKNOWLEDGMENTS

I'm grateful for Chris Casuccio, who opened that email and said yes. You made me truly believe that I could be the writer I merely dreamed I could become. Thank you for thinking that my writing deserved a home. I'm grateful for the entire team at Westwood Creative Artists for having my back.

I'm grateful for the amazing Diane Turbide, who took a chance on a first-time author who had nothing more than a blog site and some ideas on Blackness and masculinity. Thank you for allowing me to flesh out my thoughts. And believing in me.

I'm grateful for Adrienne Kerr. Your editing elevated my writing, my thought process, this book. It was a roller coaster and I'm thankful for our talks about these chapters and about the chapters of life that we both endured over the course of making this.

I'm grateful for Meredith Pal. You came on in the fourth quarter and I couldn't have asked for a better editor to sharpen my words. You championed me at a time when I desperately needed it and I am forever indebted to you.

I'm grateful for Crissy Calhoun, who put the finishing touches on this book. Your brilliance is evident.

I'm grateful for the squad at Penguin, who made me feel like an author before I became one. I had so many doubts before I went down this artistic path. I was only able to land because of you.

I'm grateful for Kiese Laymon, who showed me what Black art can look like outside of sixteens and songs and jumpshots. Reading your work *actually* changed my life, brother.

I'm grateful for the educators I've been fortunate enough to work alongside, and for all the students I've had the opportunity to teach over the last decade, who inspired me to look deeper and re-evaluate everything I thought I knew. I've learned so much from all of you. Hopefully I have paved a better path for you in return.

To everyone who I named in the book, thank you. You helped me along this lifelong journey of seeking clarity.

Mom, writing this felt like bringing you back to life. And Dad, I lost you along the way but if it wasn't for you, I wouldn't be me.

We're all searching for answers. If there's one that I hope this book teases out, it's that we each have to come up with our own.